A fifty-year history…

Other Books by Peter Viemeister

The Lightning Book:
The Nature of Lightning and How to Protect Yourself

History of Aviation: *They Were There*

Start All Over: *An American's Experience*

Peaks of Otter: *Life and Times*

From Slaves to Satellites: *250 Years of Changing Times*

The Beale Treasure: *NEW History of a Mystery*

Confederate Treasure Coverup: *Duty, Honor and Deceit*

Disinformation

CIA, JFK, TWA, 9/11...

a search for truth
& what to do

Peter Viemeister

2006

HAMILTON'S • BEDFORD • VIRGINIA • 24523

To
my children, and their children

FIRST EDITION

Copyright 2006 Peter Viemeister

All rights reserved. No part of this publication may be used or reproduced in any manner, electronic, magnetic, mechanical or optical, or transmitted or stored by any information storage and retrieval system without written permission from the publisher except in the case of brief quotations embodied in critical articles and reviews where credit is given.

First printing: October 2006

3 5 7 9 10 8 6 4 2

Published by:
Hamilton's
P.O. Box 932
Bedford, VA 24523

ISBN: 1-883912-19-9

Printed in the United States of America

Preface

This book began in 1996 after the destruction of TWA Flight 800 off Long Island where I grew up. From early boyhood, I was fascinated with airplanes and after college joined a company where I could be involved with them every day. This explosion of a proven 747 airplane in clear skies made no sense to me.

While exploring this tragedy, I became more aware of other occasions in recent history where official explanations did not always make sense.

In my seventy-seven years I grew to understand much of what went on—about people, about government, about business, and about secrets ... and of the underlying forces of personal ambition and the invisible hand of economics.

Many opportunities brought me along. An engineering degree at Rensselaer taught me how to learn. A Fellowship to the Sloan School of Management at MIT broadened my perspective during an intense year of classes, projects and travel. We Sloan Fellows met leaders in New York, Washington, London, Paris, Prague, and Moscow; I chaired the meeting at the *New York Times*, probing top editors and business managers.

In almost three decades with Grumman, a multibillion dollar aerospace company, as a design engineer, head of corporate planning, assistant to the President and Chairman of the Board during the development of the lunar module program, President of Grumman Data Systems, and later as Vice President for Development, I dealt with leaders in government, industry, finance, and pursued business as far away as Australia.

I learned about media: as head of the company's Presentations group; as my books made their way into magazines, libraries and radio and TV appearances; when elected to local office; and as a grand jury foreman.

The years enriched insight into why people do what they do. This led to inventing a simulator of human behavior, which earned a patent. I taught organizational behavior at two colleges. Dr. Harold Abramson, about whom is more in this book, helped me bridge technology and the psyche.

Service as chairman of foundations (one for community health, one for a state college system, and one for a national war memorial) and as a director on corporate and civic boards heightened my respect for ethics issues and led to implementing conflict of interest policies.

These life experiences fed my curiosity about TWA 800 and other matters of disinformation and opened windows into how things really work. This book is a result of those discoveries.

Contents

Preface 7
Chapter 1   Powers That Be 11
Chapter 2   Case Closed 17
Chapter 3   Cuba 27
Chapter 4   Camelot 35
Chapter 5   Keep Calm 43
Chapter 6   LSD Not War 49
Chapter 7   Revelations 59
Chapter 8   Iran, etc. 71
Chapter 9   Anger 77
Chapter 10   Tale of Two Sparks 85
Chapter 11   No Whistle 95
Chapter 12   Who Knew 103
Chapter 13   Homicide 111
Chapter 14   Secrets 117
Chapter 15   Persuaders 125
Chapter 16   Mind Teams 133
Chapter 17   You Choose 139
Acknowledgments 143
More Information 145
Index 151

CHAPTER ONE

Powers That Be

Coverup or not? Disinformation? What can you believe? What do you believe? Is it true?

In July 1969, hundreds of millions of people around the world watched TV and saw Neil Armstrong put his foot on the moon. It was a proud achievement for mankind. It was a thrilling moment, which would be followed by five other moon landings. Yet there are people today who don't believe it happened at all. For them, those black and white pictures are fake—a so-so TV show, like a home movie, staged in a warehouse somewhere. Kids next door make better science videos than that.

We've learned that almost any picture can be faked. Special effects made possible by powerful computers have altered the world of movies and visual images. We enjoy fantasy action—*Back to the Future* time travel automobiles, the giant *King Kong*, and medieval reconstruction of *The Da Vinci Code*—but in our hearts we know they are not real. In the courtroom, prosecutors, judges, and defendants no longer trust a photograph or a recorded voice. Entertainments have reinforced our suspicions.

History is something forgotten or never learned. Almost 140 million of today's Americans were in infancy or not yet born in 1969. They did not experience the years of space flight tests and Walter Cronkite reports, or the tense anticipation that led to the lunar landings. They only know what they have read or been taught—seemingly irrelevant like the history of Rome or Greece. Schools can only devote a brief review of the moon project. Kids are skeptical of what they are taught. What they are taught may not always be accurate.

Government has the power to make rules and to make things happen. It influences what is taught in public schools. Government decides what you are allowed to know. The media decides what you ought to know. You learn about it on TV, hear it on the radio, or read about it on the Internet or in magazines, papers or books. You learn in a classroom or from a friend or the grapevine. What you finally know is not always what you actually need to know. And what you do know is not always true.

Former U-2 spy plane pilot Carl Overstreet says that someone with enough power can make anything seem true. And then people make decisions based upon the way things seem, not the way they are. A prudent citizen voter needs to be mindful of the "powers that be."

Shakespeare reminds us that all of life is a stage. Major officials campaign to be elected for roles on the public stage. The media reviews their performances and also the developing plot. The voting public applauds or stays home. Some drama goes on back stage. Government can have legitimate secrets. Government may disguise truth with disinformation.

Many citizens do not trust our government. Many do not trust the media either. There have been too many instances where facts were withheld and untruths were told only to have the truth later emerge, leaving us convinced that we had been deceived.

Our republic comes closest to its ideals when our leaders set aside their personal motivations and aspirations and instead put in first place the needs of our nation and its people. This country is unique in the world because of its respect for individual freedom, a wisely constructed constitution for a government of checks and balances, freedom of speech, and a competitive free market for ideas and commerce. Our free press is a powerful force for what our nation has been, is now, and will be.

Americans may all be "from Missouri," being skeptical of what they read or hear. It may be something deep in the American psyche, our rural roots, the instinct to distrust strangers, those big shots, those government guys. They are not from here. Or maybe our distrust is being cultivated by the media.

It is hard to decide what is true and what isn't. Americans love watching mysteries: *NCIS*, *CSI*, detective tales, true crime reports, and whodunits. Americans are intrigued when Sam Giancana's daughter writes that Sam helped plan the JFK assassination. The Oliver Stone movie is more persuasive and more compelling than the Warren Commission document. Show business produces stories, advertisers pay to show them and we watch them. The "bad guy" is often a politician, a leader, a big business man, or the police chief. Dramatic fiction fuels our general distrust. The more we see, the more we distrust real life. Americans suspect politicians and their decisions and instead believe the critics.

Americans do not want to believe that a lone, young, ne'er-do-well in his twenties named Oswald could plan and actually kill an American president. That's too simple. They do not want to believe that a tiny spark in a fuel tank can make a jumbo jet explode and kill 230 people. They do not want to believe that a White House counsel shot himself in the Marcy Park. They do not want to believe that Marilyn Monroe killed herself.

They have learned that things aren't always as they seem. They know that sinister forces can be at work. They are ready to believe that "powerful people" had "something to do with it." They see alarming headlines on tabloids at the checkout counter. They surf the Internet and find all kinds of conspiracy ideas which may or may not be true. Once an idea becomes embedded, a later and better one may be rejected.

Confidence in government fades and conspiracy ideas grow when facts are withheld. Government has access to facts we do not and it has the power to block access to those facts. There are situations where it is indeed best to keep a secret for the public good. Some facts remain justifiably sheltered for decades or more. Some facts which do not deserve such protection are ultimately revealed sooner. But there seem to be too many secrets.

This book examines the issue of secrecy and disinformation for several events in recent American history, in particular the assassination of John F. Kennedy, the downing of TWA Flight 800, the events of 9/11, and the death of Dr. Frank Olson.

The murder of President Kennedy in 1963 flooded the nation with sadness and left a legacy of conspiracy theories and unsolved questions. The author asked 158 individual adults at random, "The Warren Commission concluded that the killing of Kennedy was by Lee Harvey Oswald, and he alone. Do you believe that?" Five people agreed, one was ambivalent, and

152 said, "No." When asked why they did not believe it, typical explanations were, "They lie," "You can't believe what the government says," "Why should we?", "We're not as dumb as they think." No one seems able to define exactly who "they" are, those who lexicographer Anne Soukhanov calls "the great gray *they*."

The downing of TWA Flight 800 in 1996 took the lives of all 230 persons aboard. The official investigation concluded that the cause of the explosion was a spark inside the center fuel tank. Ignored were more than 100 eyewitnesses who had seen what looked like a missile rising from the surface of the water to the plane.

The attack of 9/11 in 2001 shocked Americans. Hijackers took over four airliners virtually simultaneously. Two crashed into and destroyed the World Trade Center towers, one crashed into the Pentagon, and one was headed to the White House or Capitol before crashing short in Pennsylvania. Government has the duty to protect us from hostile foes foreign or domestic. Couldn't our government have prevented this disaster? What did authorities know?

The apparent suicide of Dr. Frank Olson in 1953 was essentially unreported by the media, except for a small obituary in a local Maryland newspaper. Twenty-two years later, his death was on the front page of the *New York Times*, and a movie appeared in 2002. The mysterious death of Dr. Olson is testimony to one family's courage and dogged determination to uncover the facts and get them out into the public. In spite of a disinformation campaign and stonewalling by the powerful federal government, the Olson family persisted. Though at great personal cost, their half-century crusade gives hope that you can indeed "fight city hall."

Our democratic republic is inefficient and imperfect, but no one has yet found a better and more lasting system. Informed voters can insure that the United States of America endures.

CHAPTER TWO

Case Closed

On November 28, 1953, Dr. Frank Olson's family was informed that he had died after he had fallen or jumped from a tenth floor hotel window in New York City, an apparent suicide.

Olson was a bacteriologist employed at the United States Army's Fort (then Camp) Detrick Research Center in Maryland. His family knew little about the exact nature of his work because it was classified by the government. They were unaware that he was, in fact, working for the Central Intelligence Agency (CIA) Special Operations Division and that a summer trip to Europe was to visit a joint US-English research facility in Germany.

The family noticed that Dr. Olson was becoming depressed and sad. This depression deepened after he returned from the business trip to Europe.

His unexpected death stunned his wife Alice and their three children, Eric, 9, Lisa, 7, and Nils, 5. The family found it hard to believe what the government had told them. A loving family, the Olsons could not accept that he had taken his own life.

Critical as it was for the Olsons, this death of one man was not news; it was unnoticed by the media except for a simple newspaper obituary the next day. The press did not investigate. It was a closed casket funeral.

The true circumstances of Dr. Olson's death were obscured and not made known to the family for more than twenty-two years. Profoundly significant factors would be exposed in a government report in 1975. Only then would they learn that he had been working for the CIA and that he had been given drugs without his knowledge.

This tragedy of Frank Olson was the culmination of a series of world, national, and personal events. The United States and its allies had prevailed in winning the lengthy, global war against Germany and Japan. The chaos of years of war spawned its share of misdeeds, errors, and immoral acts of chicanery. But these were lost beneath a overwhelming plethora of inspiring deeds of courage and heroism.

The postwar years were times when the CIA operated beneath a very tight lid of secrecy. Most citizens were patriots who were proud of having won the big war. They believed that their government would do what was right. That was all they needed to know.

Only a few, a select few, Senators and Congressmen could oversee the Agency's budgets. Georgia Sen. Richard Russell, long-time Chairman of Defense Appropriations, once said that "if there is anything in the United States which should be held sacred behind the curtain of classified matter, it is information regarding the activities of this agency.... It would be better to abolish it out of hand than it would be to adopt a theory that such information should be spread and made available to every member of Congress and to the members of the staff of any committee...."

Certainly, ordinary citizens, and even families of CIA employees, were deemed to have no reason to be told what really went on.

After the end of World War II in 1946, German and Japanese leaders were brought to Nuremberg to face international tribunals where they were tried for war crimes. Haunted by the Holocaust and images of experiments upon unwilling innocents, some twenty-two top German leaders and twenty-three top Japanese leaders were found guilty of war crimes and crimes against humanity. Their convictions served notice to leaders everywhere that leaders could and should be held culpable for inhumane treatment of prisoners and innocents. World sentiment condemned the use of biological weapons.

In the United States, research into offensive and defensive use of chemical and biological weapons (CBW), begun after World War I, continued during World War II, accelerated by reports of use of such weapons by Germany and Japan. At the sprawling 1,200-acre US Army Fort Detrick, some of our brightest experts in chemistry and biology served our country in research. One such scientist, Dr. Frank Olson, joined the organization in 1943 when he was thirty-three after he had earned his PhD at the University of Wisconsin.

Certain enemy scientists were granted amnesty in exchange for revealing their special knowledge. US research continued after the war, ostensibly to strengthen the US defensive ability.

In 1947, President Harry Truman signed off on the creation of the CIA to direct and coordinate all foreign intelligence activity for national security. Because it could involve espionage and clandestine activity, it maintained a special obscurity.

North Korea invaded South Korea on June 25, 1950. President Truman committed US military forces to push them back, and three months later US forces landed at Inchon, South Korea. What was initially termed a "police action," under the aegis of the United Nations, would run for years and take 33,667 American lives.

US research included experiments with the mind-altering drug lysergic acid diethylamide (LSD). In May 1950, Dr. Max Rinkle and Dr. Robert Hyde reported that tests of LSD on 100 volunteers showed that LSD produced psychotic disturbances. By 1951, the United States had an exclusive contract to buy LSD from a Swiss pharmaceutical firm. At Detrick, the leader of project testing psychoactive drugs was Dr. Sidney Gottlieb, then thirty-three.

In the summer of 1952, North Korea reported that captured US pilots had confessed to releasing chemical/biological agents against the North. When an international committee concluded that it was true, the US denied it.

The American people respected Dwight David "Ike" Eisenhower for his leadership to victory in Europe. Their votes in November 1952 called him to duty again, as President. He was expected to resolve the Korean war.

Richard Nixon, in spite of a seeming sour and thin-skinned personality, had been reelected as a Congressman from California for being tough on communism and tough on organized crime. He aspired to the White House, and in 1952 he ran for vice president with presidential candidate Dwight Eisenhower. Republicans swept in as Ike easily beat Adlai Stevenson. Nixon, like many other vice presidents in American history, hungered to become president himself some day.

Eisenhower was sworn in as President of the United States in January 1953. Our hero was now in charge. The media and the public would trust this man. He appointed John Foster Dulles as Secretary of State and he elevated John's brother, Allen Dulles, to be Director of Central Intelligence as DCI's Gen. Bedell Smith retired.

Unknown to the public and unknown to the media, Allen Dulles approved a program, code named MKULTRA, which drew upon earlier British and German research experience with LSD. It was part of what he said was a "mind war." This project included hopes for finding ways to get prisoners to tell secrets that they didn't want to tell. Another goal was to find ways to disturb minds so that they would forget their secrets or muddle their thinking so no one would believe them. It would be delicate work: as with all matters dealing with human physiology, too much of any chemical substance can be fatal. We don't know if Dulles bothered to tell Ike about the project.

The United States in 1953 continued to engage in a Cold War with the Soviets and its satellite nations. In Asia, the war in Korea had cooled down and an armistice was signed on July 27. Simmering efforts by Britain and our CIA in Iran culminated in the ousting of Prime Minister Mohammed Mossadegh, who was moving to nationalize the oil industry facilities. He was replaced by young Mohammed Reza Shah.

During that summer, Dr. Olson visited Europe. He confided to Dr. William Sargant, a British colleague, that he was troubled by what experiments he had seen, and alluded to experiments which ended with death. Olson's soul-searching could cause him to appear a security risk.

Olson continued to work, but was depressed. He told his wife that he had made a terrible mistake and talked about leaving the Army and becoming a dentist.

November 19, 1953, Dr. Frank Olson himself became part of an experiment. He and a group of Army and CIA researchers met in a rented camp on a lake in Maryland. Dr. Gottlieb is said to have disbursed LSD into Olson's glass of Cointreau, only telling him after he had done it. Was this simply just one more experiment to see what people do or say when the mind is altered? Would the resulting behavior raise the likelihood of his speaking out, or so garble his mind that he would be incoherent and be unbelievable?

It is not known if others at the lodge received a dose, bigger or smaller, or none at all. Hundreds of people had already taken LSD in controlled settings or reported their experiences. Olson's response could well have been foreseeable.

During the ensuing days, he behaved abnormally, stumbling, very depressed, and somewhat paranoid. His colleagues concluded he needed special help, and he entered a psychiatric hospital in Maryland. Then his family was told he was going to see a specialist in New York for his depressed state. Five days after ingesting LSD, Olson was in the New York office of Dr. Harold A. Abramson, known to some as an allergist, but known to the CIA as an expert on LSD and its effects. Patient and doctor were already acquainted, having worked together on a project at Edgewood Arsenal. Each man had two young sons.

Dr. Abramson, then fifty-three, was a graduate of Columbia University. Of average height and build, Harold Abramson would not stand out in a crowd. But in conversation, he would. He had a researcher's curiosity and a scholar's memory and would speak with the quiet ease and confidence of broad experience. Patients of his psychiatric counseling found him genial and supportive. One teenager described him as "an old wise man who listened a lot."

The worldly Abramson had studied and done research in Europe, conducted LSD and psychiatric research in a New York City hospital, Edgewood Arsenal in New Jersey, and had an office on 58th Street in the City and one on Long Island. He was proud of his early exploratory research into the effects of LSD, beginning with tests of worms and fish. Harold had a connection with the Cold Spring Harbor Laboratory on Long Island, New York, where James D. Watson, Nobel winner for DNA research, did some of his genetic research.

Abramson had a home in the wooded residential area of Laurel Hollow, about one mile west of the lab. Not far to the east and one mile from the lab, up Snake Hill Road, overlooking Cold Spring Harbor waters, was the stately home of the Dulles family, with a "mother" cottage on the property.

Olson met with Abramson on four consecutive days that November. Traveling to New York with Col. Vincent Ruwet, Olson had three sessions on the 24th and one on the 25th in the city office. After the session on the 25th, Olson made a round trip to Washington and returned with colleague Robert V. Lashbrook. Then he met at Abramson's office on Long Island on the 26th, and again in New York on Friday the 27th.

Abramson's notes mentioned that Olson had had delusional events and that Olson said his inordinate guilt feelings had to do with his retirement and disability pay. "He himself dated his difficulties to the time when he retired."

We assume that Olson had actually resigned and knew the terms of his "retirement" when seeing Abramson. It is unclear if he had already resigned when given the dose of LSD at the lake on November 19 or if he was still employed at that time. Was his pension and separation compensation more or less than normal for a professional level employee after ten years on the job? He was forty-three years old.

Abramson wrote that Olson agreed to enter a mental institution near home, and plans were made for hospitalization the next day. Lashbrook and Olson shared Room 1018A in New York's Pennsylvania Hotel that evening with plans to return to Maryland in the morning.

After midnight, Olson went out the window from the tenth floor room and died on the street below. It was Saturday the 28th, just nine days after he had been dosed with LSD.

Lashbrook called Dr. Abramson, and a hotel switchboard person overheard Lashbrook say, "He's gone." He also recalled hearing Abramson say, "That's too bad."

The case was treated as a suicide. No autopsy was done.

The Olson family coped as best they could. They didn't talk about what happened. Suicide is never a comfortable subject. The children grew up not talking about it, but wondering.

The years went by.

CHAPTER THREE

Cuba

Events and issues of the next six years built the stage for the actors of the 1960's decade.

The Supreme Court decision on *Brown* vs. *Board of Education* mandated the desegregation of public schools and triggered a tide of transformation of black-white relations in America.

Progress of a more physical nature started to crisscross the country; Eisenhower pushed a huge construction program to create a national network of 44,000 miles of new interstate highways.

World War II was fading in memory, but the Cold War continued. Communism seemed to be spreading to many parts of the globe, and Washington was troubled by the growing influence of communism in Asia, in Vietnam. Eisenhower approved a small contingent of military advisors to support friendly leadership in South Vietnam. Most Americans paid no attention.

The Kennedys of Massachusetts, Lyndon B. Johnson of Texas, and the small nation of Cuba were about to grab center stage of America's interest and concerns.

Joseph P. Kennedy had the power of wealth but not the acceptance of established society. He had long hoped that some day one of his sons would be President of the United States. His oldest, Joe Jr., died during World War II. He shifted his hopes upon John, Bobby and Ted.

Joe Kennedy had become rich in financial markets and from distribution of alcoholic beverages during the bootleg era of prohibition. Legend attributes much of his success to alliances with and help from the mob.

Joe Kennedy was a big contributor to Democratic campaigns. He served President Franklin D. Roosevelt as head of the Securities and Exchange Commission. His contributions earned his appointment as US Ambassador to Britain.

He and his family lived a life of privilege. He could afford to send his children to Ivy League schools and to finance political campaigns of his sons. His financial resources helped propel son John "Jack" Kennedy (JFK), with a ready smile but an aching back, to be elected as a Massachusetts Congressman and then, in 1952, a US Senator.

Jack's 31-year-old younger brother, Robert "Bobby" Kennedy, attracted national attention as chief counsel of McClellan Committee investigating the Teamsters union in 1957. His tenacious, aggressive investigations of improprieties led to the downfall of leader Dave Beck. This opened the way for tough Jimmy Hoffa to become union chief. Thereafter, Kennedy pursued Hoffa until one of them died. Hoffa had risen through the ranks and envied and resented the young man who had come from a life of luxury. Hoffa never hid his distaste for Bobby Kennedy. He wanted to stop his probing, oust him from authority, and, reportedly, he even talked about having him killed.

Lyndon B. Johnson (LBJ), 46, of Texas was chosen as Majority Leader of the United States Senate in 1954. A tall man, with unforgettably big hands and a powerful handshake, he was a formidable politician, skilled at resolving issues by arm-twisting other politicians to compromise. He was sure of himself and readily browbeat even the most powerful of his Senate colleagues. Behind closed doors he would denigrate those opposed to him. LBJ was rarely loved, but almost always respected. He cajoled, he persuaded, and he threatened... and usually got his way. He envied the easy status of the Kennedy brothers, Senator Jack and his young lawyer brother, Bobby. Johnson relished power and wanted to be President.

Away from the political scene, scientists continued studying LSD. Some laymen got access to the chemical and experimented on themselves. A popular justification was "to explore and expand their consciousness."

The Josiah Macy, Jr. Foundation sponsored a conference for researchers in LSD therapy in 1959. Dr. Harold Abramson, the New York LSD researcher who had counseled Olson in 1953, was recording secretary. Conference Chairman Dr. Paul Hoch, associated with the CIA and Army, was unenthusiastic about the use of LSD for therapy. He opined that LSD and mescaline produce anxiety and disorganize a patient's psychic integration.

Havana, Cuba, had long been a friendly neighbor and popular port of call and vacation spot. Cruise ships, yachts, ocean ferries, airliners and private planes brought fun-seekers to Havana to savor its warm weather and hospitality, and try to beat the odds at the enticing casinos. Free of US laws, Havana was a mecca for gamblers. American organized crime controlled the industry and earned substantial profits. The incumbent ruler of Cuba derived a share also.

This thriving activity came to a halt in 1959 when Fidel Castro ousted Cuban dictator Batista, closed the casinos, and banned gambling. He briefly jailed gambling bosses and investors, including kin of Meyer Lansky and Santo Trafficante, Jr., who had fled to Cuba in 1957 to escape charges related to an organized crime conference in the US. Castro's actions kicked out organized crime and shut down their money machine.

New York Times writer H. L. Matthews was enthralled by Castro's idealism and eloquence and had been boosting his public image since 1957. He cheered the demise of Batista. The United States government, however, worried about the rise of communism just ninety miles from Florida. This toehold might spread elsewhere in the western hemisphere. Senator John Kennedy was one of many in Congress who wanted Castro out of power.

Some Cubans fled to the United States to escape the suppressions of communism. They dreamed of the day when they could rejoin relatives in a free Cuba. Outraged, however, was the syndicate. They wanted Castro out. They wanted to get back in business, the sooner the better. Neither the exiles nor the mob imagined that Fidel Castro would control Cuba for more than half a century.

Quietly, invisibly, the Eisenhower administration, the CIA, and organized crime adopted the same goal: remove Castro from power. At the White House, Vice President Nixon endorsed one way: train exiles to invade their homeland.

Eisenhower required that no American personnel be involved in the invasion.

Legend has it that DCI Allen Dulles explored with mobster Sam Giancana ways to assassinate Fidel Castro, including such ideas as exploding cigars or a possible poison pill for Castro's soda. There is no evidence that the White House authorized these assassination plots. Eisenhower's desire for "action" may have been assumed as justification of "any means" of action.

There were rumors that the CIA had been involved some way in the assassination of foreign leaders unfriendly to the US. There was no clear national policy about assassination. Cuban loyalists or Soviet agents apparently pierced the CIA security cloak; Castro learned of the plans against him and warned that any attempts against him would trigger "answer in kind."

Few Americans had wrestled with the idea or legality or morality of assassinating a foreign leader. Assassination can be a tool of a country's national defense policy. Fair game would be an enemy leader, such as Adolph Hitler, during time of war. However, here was a rumor that the US was entertaining plans to assassinate the leader of Cuba, against whom there was no declaration of war. The Constitution says that it is for Congress to declare war, and Congress had not done so about Cuba.

Does the blanket term "national security" justify the assassination of a visitor within the United States? A US citizen? Can our own domestic law enforcement forces assassinate a United States citizen without trial? Should the police be allowed to assign a sniper the task of killing a known gang leader who has not been indicted or convicted? Under what circumstances could it be justified and, importantly, who should have the authority to decide? These questions would float through the minds of thoughtful lawmakers for some years, with no answer.

Neither the United States nor Russia trusted the other. Russia was very protective of its military activity and banned foreigners from seeing military facilities and factories. Tourist were prohibited from taking pictures. The Russians misled everyone by inaccurate maps which distorted highway routes and mislocated or omitted important landmarks. We wanted to see more.

The CIA sponsored the secret development of a unique, high-altitude spy plane with supersensitive cameras which could overfly Russia and photograph significant sites. It was the U-2, a glider-like plane with a powerful jet engine, created by Lockheed in its secret "Skunk Works" in California and tested at Area 51 in Nevada. The very first plane made its first experimental flight in 1955. These planes and their crews would later be termed "collectors" for the National Security Agency (NSA).

Less than a year later, on June 20, 1956, a U-2 made the first "hot flight" over the Iron Curtain, flying far higher than any Russian interceptor planes and above the reach of defensive missiles. Carl Overstreet, a Virginian with Air Force jet fighter experience over Korea, piloted that mission. He said, "It must have been frustrating for the Russians—knowing that we were up there and being unable to do anything about it."

Shortly after Overstreet's flight, Carmine Vito piloted a U-2 over Moscow. Many flights followed, each approved by the White House. Almost four years elapsed before the Soviets were able to field a missile which could reach up to a U-2. Meanwhile, the American public knew nothing of the U-2 project. But Russian air defenders knew all too well every time a U-2 flew over. We said nothing. They said nothing.

On May 1, 1960, a Russian missile finally brought down a U-2. The Russians protested vigorously. President Eisenhower denied any US knowledge. But then, Khruschev showed wreckage photos and announced that the pilot, Gary Powers, had survived and was in custody. The embarrassed Eisenhower had to reverse his story. The American people then learned that there was such a thing as a U-2. The enemy had known it for years, but did not know its precise capabilities.

Soviet Premier Nikita Khruschev continued to duel with American presidents by stretching the reach of communism and by testing America's resolve. For him, Cuba was an opportunity. Cuba could be a test of how far he could push.

The Russians had nurtured Fidel Castro's revolution and then supported it by buying Cuban products. Russian agents apparently were tracking the plans of exiles to retake control of Cuba.

CHAPTER FOUR

Camelot

Senator John Fitzgerald Kennedy, "JFK," won the Democratic nomination for president in 1960, beating Lyndon Johnson. Compared to the retiring President Eisenhower, 70, who had survived heart attacks, and Vice President Nixon, Massachusetts Senator Jack Kennedy, 43, was the image of youth and vigor. The public adored his stylish and seemingly shy wife, Jacqueline Bouvier Kennedy, "Jackie." Americans relished stories and press coverage about this charming couple. Off camera, JFK was dogged by asthma and painful back problems. Media knew, but reported little, about the less than ideal marriage relationship and rumors of the President's adventurous extramarital affairs.

During the first-ever televised presidential debates, Kennedy spoke with zest and conviction. Nixon looked sour and grim. Nixon lost by 118,550 votes out of a total popular vote of 68,335,642—a margin of less than one quarter of one percent.

Organized crime boss Sam Giancana privately claimed some credit for helping Illinois carry for Kennedy. Nixon fretted as he realized that even if the debatable tally in Illinois flipped to his favor, Kennedy would still have more electoral votes. He decided not to protest and began hoping to someday have another chance.

After the election, Ike made a farewell address warning America to beware of the influence of the powerful military-industrial complex. He then traded center stage for the quiet life at his farm in Gettysburg, Pennsylvania.

The media and the public looked to the future with optimism. It would be a hopeful time for America.

John F. Kennedy took the oath of office as President of the United States in January 1961. Father Joe had realized his dream at last. New Vice President Lyndon Johnson and former Vice President Richard Nixon would wait for a turn.

After the formal ceremonies and gala, when no TV cameras were watching, Jack, Jackie, and Jackie's close cousin Mike Bouvier explored the White House living quarters together. Jackie Bouvier and Mike Bouvier were more than cousins—more like siblings having lived in the same house when growing up. Mike, a gentle gentleman, with a nice smile beneath his small black mustache, told the author about this "tour." The three of them gawked at each room and sometimes bounced on the beds. Visualize this—John Fitzgerald Kennedy was leader of the most powerful country in the world, but on this tour he was still a little boy at heart.

Father Joe convinced JFK to appoint younger brother, Bobby, as Attorney General. Vice President Johnson disliked the choice but accepted the President's right to choose. Certainly, if LBJ were President, he would choose someone else. The choice of Secretary of Defense was former Ford Motor Company executive, Robert S. McNamara. Top military brass were cool to this man who relied on staff "whiz kids" who used numbers to evaluate alternative military options. For Secretary of State, Kennedy chose Dean Rusk.

The Kennedy brothers were unsure about both the FBI and the CIA intelligence organizations. They had learned that the CIA was much more than "intelligence." L. Fletcher Prouty, former Chief of Special Operations for the Joint Chiefs of staff, called the CIA "the center of a vast, amorphous mechanism that specializes in covert operations."

Centuries ago, Francis Bacon said, "Knowledge is power," and leaders in government everywhere are ever mindful of this truth. When President Harry Truman signed the National Security Act of 1947, leery of creating a US domestic Gestapo, he created the Central Intelligence Agency for external matters only and, expressly, no internal security functions. The Act assigned internal security and counter espionage to the Federal Bureau of Investigation. The mass of information accumulated over the years and held close by the Bureau provided its leadership with important power. Over in the CIA, there were other vast files of information, held close by its leadership. The CIA and FBI often sparred to strengthen and protect their own informational territory as the boundaries of authority sometimes overlapped or blurred. Kennedy kept J. Edgar Hoover over the FBI and replaced Allen Dulles at the CIA with a man of his choice, John A. McCone.

The Kennedys were warily impressed by what the FBI admitted it knew about their private lives. They wondered what else the FBI knew and what the CIA was doing. Bobby Kennedy once remarked that the FBI chief was "dangerous." FBI boss J. Edgar Hoover had said he hated Bobby. Its very name, Central Intelligence Agency, does not imply that it is an action organization, such as the Army, Navy, or Air Force. In reality, it had done more than collect information. The CIA worried that the Kennedys might diminish its mission and authority or give it to the Department of Defense, which had its own intelligence organizations and professional operation action capability. Both the FBI and the CIA jealously guarded their secrets from the nation's enemies and from each other, a situation that continued well into 2001, as the nation later learned from the 9/11 Commission hearings.

In reality, the Kennedys and the country needed both intelligence organizations to help see the total picture.

Secrets are not very secret if too many people know them. Plans to invade Cuba apparently leaked out to Cuba and, probably, to its mentor Russia.

In April 1961, the Cuban dissidents would finally attempt their invasion. The exiles had expected US air cover. It is unclear if that expectation was an actual promise or just a presumption.

It is clear that Castro had learned what was coming. He amassed his military defense forces on the shore, ready. He and his Russian supporters both knew. It is probable too that the US knew of the Cuban defense buildup. The Russians may have warned the US that they would give full support to Castro, or perhaps the Kennedys realized that US involvement could mean facing the Russians. JFK and his cabinet were not ready for a big war.

On invasion day, April 17, 1961, the US stood back and watched. The Russians watched, too. Castro's forces outnumbered the invaders, there was no air cover, and the invasion of Cuba at the Bay of Pigs was a disastrous failure. The CIA, who had been actively involved in the planning and undercover work, was burdened with blame. Other fingers pointed at the exiles. Some blamed the White House. Castro stood prouder and stronger than before.

The mob was disappointed.

The Russians also claimed the lead in space technology: Yuri Gagarin became the first man to orbit the world.

Kennedy wanted to take back the lead. He decided the US should go to the moon, a brave and daring challenge. In May 1961, he said, "I believe that this nation should commit itself to achieving the goal, before this decade is out, of landing a man on the Moon and returning him safely to Earth. No single space project in this period will be more impressive to mankind, or more important in the long range exploration of space; and none shall be so difficult or expensive to accomplish." This commitment may have forestalled any war with Russia. Instead of posturing with armies and navies, the two nations would direct their resources to compete and win, not a battle of destruction, but a race for eminence in the new frontier of space.

The Bay of Pigs failure emboldened the Russians and Cuba to challenge America again. The next summer, the US learned that Russia started building a base on Cuba for surface-to-surface guided missiles which could reach the United States mainland. High-flying U-2's photographed the buildup.

In mid-October, treetop-level F101 reconnaissance planes captured images of missile equipment being unloaded from cargo planes and Soviet ships bringing missiles toward Cuba. Pictures were whisked to the White House, and President Kennedy on October 22nd appeared on television to report what was happening. He ordered a naval and air quarantine of shipments.

Broadcast media kept the world informed, minute by minute. Americans sat by their TV's—wondering if there would be a nuclear showdown. Some homeowners stocked up on food. Engineer Robert Lyons, recalling World War II shortages, bought a new car.

Ominous messages were exchanged between Khruschev and the White House. President Jack, counseled by Attorney General Bobby, Defense Secretary McNamara and Rusk of State, developed a compromise which was announced on the 28th. The US would not invade Cuba and the Russians would withdraw the missiles. Kennedy had faced the adversary and won. Americans relaxed.

There was another oblique angle to the deal, not officially part of the deal, not so well known: former Secretary of Defense McNamara has said that the US decided to withdraw US missiles from Turkey. This was not part of the agreement, he said; the missiles were old anyway and "it was not an agreement, it was a statement of unilateral decision."

The Russians had shed a threat to their homeland. Castro had a renewed lease on life, safe from American invasion. There may have been a tacit understanding that the Soviets would take no military action so long as we left their "boy" alone.

Organized crime made no deal with the Russians. Operating outside (or under) the law, they might still try to assassinate the Cuban leader. The Kennedy brothers had mixed emotions about being part of that. The mob once had a role in the Kennedy family prosperity. There was some sense of obligation for help which the family had received. The US would indeed be better off if the mob did make it happen. They could be on the same "side" with Giancana about Castro, but they could not take an active part and dared not risk being blamed for the death of Castro.

The mob was disappointed again. After helping the elder Kennedy get rich and JFK get elected, they were not getting help in restoring their Cuban business. And, too, they faced a Kennedy Attorney General aggressively prosecuting their organization. They smoldered.

But Fidel Castro eluded potential assassinators. He continued to breathe and to boss Cuba, and would do so into the next century.

Castro had prevailed. The Russians showed they could shake up the world. Philip Graham, publisher of *Newsweek* and the *Washington Post,* met often as an advisor to the Kennedy brothers and was an enthusiastic booster of Kennedy's Apollo space exploration program. He married Katherine Meyer, daughter of *Post* publisher Eugene Meyer, who later became president of the World Bank.

Graham developed emotional problems. He was committed to Chestnut Lodge, released, recommitted and released again. On August 3, 1963, he apparently shot himself. Katherine took over the publications.

Vice President Johnson, who had chaired the National Space Council, championed the Apollo project and a role for his home state of Texas. The administration announced that the Apollo space program would be headquartered at the new Johnson Manned Space Center in Houston.

Texas would also be the scene of one of the most puzzling assassinations in the US ever. Two men had crucial roles in this event: Lee Harvey Oswald and Jack Ruby.

Among the denizens of the city of Dallas was Jack Ruby, 52, one of eight children of a Russian immigrant, operator of a small nightclub. Ruby was a bumblebee who hung out with police and underworld characters alike. A walking data bank of netherworld information, he enjoyed giving the impression that he was more important than he was.

Lee Harvey Oswald, 24, a recent resident of Dallas, was a loser who failed to succeed in America's free enterprise capitalist system. He was court-martialed and left the US Marines. He visited Russia, renounced his American citizenship, and was allowed to live there, where he met his bride, Marina. In short time, he became disillusioned with life under communism and somehow got approval to return to America. He publicly espoused the cause of Castro's Cuba and tried to return to Russia via Cuba. In Texas, in April 1963, he took a shot at arch conservative Major General Edwin A. Walker, but missed. He made visits to New Orleans and to Mexico City. On November 22, 1963, he left his apartment with a long box wrapped in brown paper and went to his menial job at the Texas School Book Depository.

That day, a presidential motorcade would pass by.

CHAPTER FIVE

Keep Calm

Kennedy was shot November 22, 1963 at 1:30 P.M.

Reporter Tom Wicker wrote the first report in a copyright *New York Times* article:

> *Dallas, Nov. 22—President John Fitzgerald Kennedy was shot and killed by an assassin today.*
>
> *He died of a wound in the brain caused by a rifle bullet that was fired at him as he was riding through downtown Dallas in a motorcade.*
>
> *Vice President Lyndon Baines Johnson, who was riding in the third car behind Mr. Kennedy's, was sworn in as the 36th President of the United States 99 minutes after Mr. Kennedy's death.*

Police arrested Lee Harvey Oswald and accused him of the killing. Two days later, Jack Ruby shot and killed Oswald in the police station. All the TV stations showed what happened.

People hungered to know why. Creative minds tried to explain this seemingly unthinkable event; they conceived of conspiracies. Rumors spread that it was a left-wing conspiracy—or a right-wing conspiracy, there was more than one gunman, that "the Mafia" did it, that Castro and Russia were behind it, the CIA, LBJ....

Unlike Jack Kennedy, Lyndon Johnson was not adored by the public or the press. LBJ was a tough politician. It was no secret that he wanted to be President. Now, suddenly he was indeed President. Johnson, a master practitioner of politics, knew he would have to win public confidence in an election in 1964, less than a year away, if he wanted to stay in office as President.

Johnson rushed to get the facts and calm the country down. He and J. Edgar Hoover developed a list of people to serve on a commission to investigate, with Supreme Court Justice Earl Warren to be chairman.

Warren was reluctant to serve. But LBJ persuaded him. You are the right man. We don't have time to search around.

If he believed that Castro was behind the shooting, Johnson could have chosen to let Cuba take the blame, but that might ignite public clamor to attack Cuba. Mindful of the recent US deal with Russia, LBJ believed that any attack on Cuba would surely provoke Russia to help Cuba and then perhaps strike the US. LBJ was firm that we must avoid such chaos. Besides it would be very disruptive during a presidential election campaign.

LBJ issued Executive order #11130, November 29, 1963, to establish a commission to investigate the assassination of President Kennedy. In addition to Chairman Earl Warren, the members were Senators Richard B. Russell and John Sherman Cooper, Representatives Hale Boggs and Gerald Ford, Mr. Allen W. Dulles and Mr. John J. McCloy. General Counsel would be J. Lee Rankin.

The Commission met for the first time December 5, 1963. It searched for answers during the ensuing ten months. Meanwhile, rumors, public moods and beliefs became frozen and preset.

The Commission conveyed its report to Johnson on September 24, 1964:

> *Your Commission to investigate the assassination of President Kennedy on November 22, 1963, having completed its assignment in accordance with Executive Order No. 11130 of November 29, 1963, herewith submits its final report.*

LBJ released the full report in early October. Within just eighty hours, in an awesome display of publication prowess, the *New York Times* and Bantam Books made available to the public 700,000 copies. It was a big report. The printed version covered more than 700 pages. It was an instant best seller. All major media helped communicate the findings.

The Commission's conclusions included these key points:

- The shots which killed President Kennedy and wounded Governor Connally were fired from the sixth floor window.

- The nature of the bullet wounds suffered by President Kennedy and Governor Connally and the location of the car at the time of the shots establish that the bullets were fired from above and behind the Presidential limousine.

- There is no credible evidence that the shots were fired from the Triple Underpass, ahead of the motorcade, or from any other location.

- The weight of the evidence indicates that there were three shots fired.

- No direct or indirect relationship between Lee Harvey Oswald and Jack Ruby has been discovered by the Commission, nor has it been able to find any credible evidence that either knew the other, although a thorough investigation was made of the many rumors and speculations of such a relationship.

- The Commission has found no evidence that Jack Ruby acted with any other person in the killing of Lee Harvey Oswald.

Lyndon Johnson had fervently hoped that prompt investigation by a distinguished commission would put the matter to rest. But the public didn't buy it.

An early skeptic was Bertrand Russell, noted British historian and social philosopher. One of hundreds who criticized the findings of the Commission, Russell organized a "Who Killed Kennedy Committee" of people "eminent in the intellectual life of the country." The group included a bishop, professors, publishers, authors, members of Parliament, and editors. Russell wrote "16 Questions on the Assassination" on September 6, 1964, weeks before the commission report was released.

His questions included this: "If, as we are told, Oswald was the lone assassin, where is the issue of national security?.... If the Government is so certain of its case, why has it conducted all its inquiries in the strictest secrecy?"

Many dismissed Russell's views, pointing out that he was ninety-two years old, and in his dotage. But his argument resonated with those who distrust government, any government. He said, "No US television program or mass circulation newspaper has challenged the permanent basis of all the allegations—that Oswald was the assassin, and that he acted alone. It is a task which is left to the American people."

The public found it hard to accept that a lone young man could so shake up the entire country. They wondered who was really behind it all. Who wanted Kennedy dead?

Could it have been Castro in revenge for plans to kill him and because of the Bay of Pigs and for losing his missile powers? What about Russia, which wanted to protect Castro and avenge loss of face during the missile crisis?

Or maybe one mobster, angry because he believed JFK was sleeping with his girlfriend?

Or maybe the mob, which had helped the Kennedy family in earlier years, resentful for the Kennedy's failure to oust Castro and for continued prosecutions of organized crime?

Or maybe Nixon, who wanted the deck cleared for a future presidential run? Or maybe LBJ himself, who didn't want to wait for his chance at being top man? Or the CIA, who had sensed that Kennedy would reduce its authority? Or? Or?

Aside from all this speculation, several questions of fact persisted. If Oswald was the only shooter, how likely is it that he got off three shots from his aged bolt-action rifle so quickly, so well, at a target moving away from 177 to 266 feet? If the only shots came from behind the motorcade, why did Kennedy's head snap backwards or sideways? And what about the men some say were on the grassy knoll ahead of the motorcade? Of the bullets which hit the President, how could a single bullet account for so many wounds of JFK and Governor Connally?

And what about Jack Ruby? Did he kill Oswald for his own personal reason? Ruby was jailed and charged with killing Oswald. He was convicted on March 14, 1964. While appealing the verdict, he remained in jail and died in prison in January 1967 of a pulmonary embolism. If he had done the deed for someone else, he never told anyone. Acquaintances said that Ruby was not a man who could keep secrets.

There were complaints that considerable testimony and research findings were to be sealed for decades, kept hidden from public inspection. Was this purely to protect innocent persons? Many facts became accessible as a result of the Assassination Materials Disclosure Act in 1992. The remainder are still sealed until 2017. When all these facts are finally released, perhaps the Commission's conclusions will be more acceptable.

The Commission report is available at most libraries. You can read it yourself.

CHAPTER SIX

LSD Not War

America was becoming less conservative. Traditional values and family relations deteriorated. Women were becoming free of constraint. Conception of children could be avoided with the new birth control pill. Betty Friedan's book *The Feminine Mystique* encouraged women to look outside the home and maximize their potential.

Respect for authority was deteriorating. Promoters of "alternate life style" fueled the trend with catch phrases like "if you dig it, do it" and "break the rules." The Beatles challenged the status quo and encouraged tolerance of drug use.

A favorite of this movement was Dr. Timothy Leary. A former Harvard psychology teacher, Leary advocated experimentation with LSD and personally lived his slogan, "turn on, tune in, drop out." Richard Nixon believed that Leary was the most dangerous man in America.

Desegregation moved ahead, but slowly. Martin Luther King Jr. gave his historic "I have a dream" speech in 1963 before a huge crowd in Washington, DC.

Vietnam was a war that was not an official war. Our military involvement in Vietnam had grown. Yet Congress had not formally declared war. The US initiated covert forays against shore line assets of the enemy. President Johnson authorized US forces to attack any force that attacked them.

In the first weeks of August 1964, there were reports that the US Navy destroyer, *Maddox*, had been attacked by North Vietnamese vessels in international waters in the Gulf of Tonkin. The facts were ambiguous at best. The captain and overflying naval aircraft were uncertain if there had been attacks at all. Nevertheless, the Defense Department and the President alluded to "repeated attacks" and a "second deliberate attack" and persuaded both houses of Congress on August 7th to pass the "Gulf of Tonkin Resolution" authorizing US forces to take all necessary measures to prevent further aggression. Senator Wayne Morse did not buy it, arguing that facts did not substantiate it. But the media accepted it. And the Administration used the Resolution to justify escalating into what was war.

Americans worried about nuclear war with the Soviet Union. Young men worried about that possibility and they also worried about Vietnam. During the fall of 1964, a Democratic TV campaign spot pictured a small girl with a flower and a nuclear explosion and implied that Republican candidate Barry Goldwater could be trigger happy. LBJ won easily.

Once in office as an elected president, Johnson flexed his extraordinary skills to establish his "Great Society" programs to aid the needy and uplift the disadvantaged. He believed that the country could afford it, in spite of the growing "bubble" in the budget needed to finance the war. He chose his own Attorney General, Nicholas Katzenbach. Bobby Kennedy left the Cabinet, ran for public office, and was elected a United States Senator from New York.

Critics called for the US to withdraw from Vietnam. College students staged disruptive protests on college campuses. A favorite slogan was "Make love, not war."

In February 1968, the Viet Cong staged a coordinated attack on thirty provincial capitals of South Vietnam on the same day in what became known as the Tet Offensive. The media campaigned for US withdrawal. At home, turbulence came to a boil in 1968.

Martin Luther King Jr. was on a balcony of his hotel room in Memphis, Tennessee, on April 4 when he was assassinated by a man with a rifle. No special Commission investigated. Shooter James Earl Ray was caught, tried, convicted, and imprisoned, where he later died.

New York Senator Robert Kennedy, the former US Attorney General, began campaigning for president. He was celebrating his victory in the California Democratic primary on June 5 when he was assassinated. Sirhan Sirhan fired multiple shots from a .22 caliber pistol at close range.

Sirhan, 24, was a Palestinian refugee who liked John Kennedy's compassion for the refugees, but disliked Senator Bobby Kennedy for voting to approve a sale of jet fighters to Israel. Sirhan asserted that the shooting was his own idea. He was convicted and sentenced to prison for life.

Huge crowds marched to protest the war in Vietnam. Activist organizers, some sharing different organization names but using the same mail address, refined their advocacy skills with carefully staged demonstrations for TV news cameras.

Late in the summer of 1968, incumbent President Johnson, acutely aware of his unpopularity and frustrated from being unable to resolve the national unrest, decided that he would not stand for reelection.

In Chicago, the streets around the Democratic National Convention hall erupted with demonstrations. Chicago police strong-armed the protesters under the fascinated eyes of national television viewers. The Democrats chose Johnson's vice president, Hubert Humphrey, to be their candidate in the election that fall.

Humphrey was soundly trounced. Eisenhower's former vice president, Richard Nixon, finally came out on top. Johnson retired to his Texas ranch believing that the profound and costly Great Society legislation was the right thing to do.

The biggest event of nontraditional behavior was "Woodstock" in August 1969 in Sullivan County, New York. Some 450,000 uninhibited souls jammed highways to pack into a farm pasture for a weekend concert and (what became) a free love festival. One then-19-year-old recalled, "Fantastic ... even though the mud in some places was waist deep." Woodstock was colorful and photographable. Newspapers, magazines and TV loved it. Woodstock and the Woodstock generation made history.

A *Time* magazine cover, in big print, asked, "Is God Dead?" President Nixon agonized over the evolving changes of American culture.

Battle casualties in Vietnam continued to grow. Nixon authorized aerial bombing. Believing "no light at the end of the tunnel," the media escalated its criticism of the war.

There had been a rash of bomb scares in the news. An incident on Long Island, New York, is an example of how leaders make decisions in conditions of uncertainty.

When an anonymous phone call warned that a bomb was to go off in an unspecified building of the Grumman Corporation aerospace complex in Bethpage, New York, security people immediately notified Board Chairman, E. Clinton Towl. Grumman had not been targeted before. Towl took no chances. He decided to order everyone out and then search all the buildings.

The almost 20,000 employees idled two hours in the parking lots while buildings were scoured. Production of Navy and Army aircraft halted. Work on the national Apollo moon project halted. Finally, the search ended. No bomb. Everyone went back to work. The event was widely reported by the local radio and newspapers. The hoaxer must have been elated.

A few days later, another anonymous phone call warned of a bomb. Towl conferred with plant and county security leaders and decided: high probability it is a hoax or a prank. He weighed the risk that someone could get hurt if he was wrong. He suspected that if he cleared out the facility again, there would be no end of prank calls. As a head man must, he made the decision. Ignore the call. Make no announcement. Keep working. The day passed uneventfully. No bomb. No one hurt. No news. No more bomb threats. That anonymous phone call was a non-story. The media didn't know about it. The media didn't report it.

A more significant story burst open in early 1971. *New York Times* publisher, "Punch," Arthur Ochs Sulzberger, and managing editor A.M. Rosenthal were influential pacesetters for America's news media. What they printed on the front page of the *Times* often became the lead story on evening TV network news. Mindful that they would stir up controversy, they nevertheless began printing sections of the so-called "Pentagon Papers," a 7,000-page government-sponsored analysis of the Vietnam situation which Defense Department employee Daniel Ellsberg had given to the paper. The Administration believed that the information was too sensitive and immediately sought to enjoin the *Times* from printing it. Appeals went up to the US Supreme Court. By ruling that the government failed to prove its case for keeping the "Papers" secret, the Court bolstered the right of the press to "bare the secrets of government and inform the people."

A scandal, now known as "Watergate," bubbled to the surface prior to the presidential campaign of 1972. Republican operatives, in search of Democratic party plans, broke into offices in the Watergate building. A trail of clues led to the White House. President Nixon denied knowing anything about it and began to cover it up. Nixon's enemies, as well as idealists in pursuit of truth, began accumulating evidence. Nevertheless, Nixon handily won reelection.

As Nixon entered his second term in January 1973, fighting in Vietnam finally ended when peace pacts were signed in Paris. The last US troops came out on March 29th. Finally, Vietnam was over. But Nixon's problems mounted.

Arab oil-producing nations stopped exporting oil to the United States in retaliation for US support of Israel in the Arab-Israeli War. Americans skimped with less fuel and paid higher prices for five frustrating months before the embargo ended.

Vice President Spiro Agnew was forced to resign after it became clear he had violated tax laws when he was Maryland Governor. Nixon picked a former House colleague, Michigan Congressman Gerald Ford, to be his new vice president. Ford, Minority Leader of the House, was respected by both parties and was easily confirmed as vice president.

Watergate ultimately brought down Richard Nixon in August 1974. Lying, stonewalling, and obstructing justice led to the beginning of the impeachment process. Nixon avoided it: he quit. For the first time in American history, a US President had resigned.

Vice President Ford automatically ascended to the presidency; the US had its first-ever, non-elected President. Ford promptly pardoned Nixon. Once again, the nation needed a vice president. This time, it was President Ford who nominated the new vice president. Nelson Rockefeller, who had served four terms as governor of the State of New York, got the job. Ford's White House was managed by Chief of Staff Donald Rumsfeld, a former four-term Congressman, and Deputy Assistant to the President Richard Cheney, another House colleague.

A subdued Richard Nixon, out of power, took little consolation from the fact that his old nemesis, Soviet Premier Nikita Khruschev, was also out of power, replaced by Leonid Breschnev. Caretaker President Ford would deal with a sensitive national concern.

A *New York Times* front page article shook up the Washington scene anew on December 22nd. Seymour Hersh reported that the CIA had involved itself in domestic affairs against the antiwar forces and had violated its statutory limitations. The

White House, recovering from the Nixon turmoil, prepared for a new siege. About a week later, President Ford, who had seen LBJ move quickly after JFK was shot and who had served on the Warren Commission, moved quickly to issue an executive order to establish a blue ribbon panel to look into those charges.

Ford assigned Nelson Rockefeller to head the "Commission on CIA Activities in The United States" to investigate improper activity of the CIA, including the possibility that the CIA had some sort of role in the assassination of John F. Kennedy. They would revisit the Warren Commission record on key questions. Did Oswald act alone? Were there other shooters? Why did JFK's head snap rearward or sideways after being shot from behind?

Distinguished personages were members of the Commission, including union leader Lane Kirkland, banker Douglas Dillon, General Lyman Lemnitzer, and California Governor Ronald Reagan. The President's Commission began its deliberations promptly in January, just a month after the *Times* article appeared.

Congress decided to do its own investigation of the CIA. Before January was over, the United State Senate set up a committee, chaired by Senator Frank Church, to study the US intelligence activities and possible abuses. And a few weeks after that, in mid-February, the House of Representatives created its own Select Committee on Intelligence. It was briefly chaired by Michigan Congressman Lucien Nedzi, but finally chaired by fellow Democrat Otis G. Pike from Riverhead, New York. With degrees from Princeton and Columbia, earned after serving as a Marine Corps pilot during the war in the Pacific, Pike was elected to Congress in 1961, after having been a lawyer and a justice of the peace. This crew-cut veteran stood tall and firm. These investigations would break through the stone walls which had hidden decades of heavy secrets.

CHAPTER SEVEN

Revelations

Accustomed to being virtually immune to criticism, safe behind a shroud of obscurity and overseen by very few selected senior officials of Congress and the White House, the CIA now found itself under intense scrutiny. The administration tried to temper the probing and argued that there already was adequate oversight of the CIA: a watchdog panel, the so-called "40" group (named for the meeting room number), met regularly to keep an eye on things. Secretary of State Henry Kissinger had been the recent chairman of their meetings. Congress wanted to know more. The Commission and Congressional hearings provided grist for the media mill and intrigue for the public appetite.

The Rockefeller Commission hurried and won the report race: they issued theirs in June 1975. They had reexamined the Warren Commission facts and interviewed new witnesses and gathered more recent data, but concurred with the original basic verdict. They found no conspiracy. They found no relationship of the CIA with Oswald or with Ruby. They exonerated the CIA from having a role in JFK's death.

In the matter of multiple shooters and the rumor that former CIA agent E. Howard Hunt and co-Watergate burglar Frank Sturgis had been seen on the grassy knoll on that fateful day in Dallas, the Commission concluded that they had not been there; they accepted testimony from relatives that the two men had been elsewhere. Many parade watchers had taken photos as Kennedy passed by; none of the pictures revealed any gunmen on the knoll.

They accepted the explanation of respected physicians and neurologists that the motion of Kennedy's head after being shot was an involuntary response, a neuromuscular seizure that can happen at the instant of death.

The Commission was also critical of the CIA and its drug testing, which had ended in 1967. The selling of LSD became a felony in 1968. The extent of American research and testing of chemical and biological weapons (CBW) was unknown to the public and probably unknown to most of Congress for decades. More of the story oozed to reveal that the work included research in toxic and biological substances such as anthrax and, in some instances, field tests which dispersed out of doors in remote locations to measure spread patterns and effects.

It is conceivable that an outdoor test had been made within the Western US. In the late 1950's, there was a report that a powerful lightning strike killed more than 500 sheep in a remote rocky part of Utah. This seemed most unusual, but the story was accepted as fact. Now, in the 21st century, we might wonder if that story was disinformation, intended to deflect learning the actual cause. It is possible that the sheep were Cold War victims or test specimens which had been grazing on or near the vast Dugway Proving Grounds in Utah.

A June 11th, 1975, *Washington Post* story reported that the Rockefeller Commission said, "As part of a program to test the influence of drugs on humans, research included the administration of LSD to persons who were unaware that they were being tested. This was clearly illegal. One person died in 1953, apparently as a result."

That person was Dr. Frank Olson, himself a Detrick research scientist. Back in 1953, his death was not news. There was then only a brief obituary in a Maryland local paper. Now Olson's death would become front page news.

The Olson family had been led to believe that he had committed suicide. They had not been told that he had been dosed with LSD. Now, here, was revelation about the cause and the effect. They decided to go public with their outrage and on July 10th held a press conference about the fact that the one "person" was Frank Olson. They suggested that they might sue the government for causing his death.

On July 11th, the *New York Times* published an in-depth Olson story by Joseph B. Treaster. He had interviewed people who were involved in the case in 1953. He uncovered facts from the original police report by Detective James W. Ward, in which Robert Lashbrook said he was asleep and was awakened by a crash of glass and realized that Olson was not in bed. The Olson family said that the widow had been told that Lashbrook had seen Olson running toward the window.

Did Olson jump? Was he pushed?

Treaster's story ran on the front page, which the White House reads religiously every day.

The CIA and the White House worried that possible litigation might flush out information best kept out of sight. White House attorney Rodney Hills advised that a court could well determine that Olson did not die in the course of his official duties and that his job was so sensitive that "the CIA and the Counsel's office both strongly recommend that the evidence concerning his employment not be released in a civil trial." It could well mean that there could be no effective defense against an Olson lawsuit. Hills made no reference to the "state secret privilege" concept which was cited in a case following the 9/11 disaster to block release of information.

Accusations had been made that the US used biological weapons in the Korean conflict decades earlier. The United States steadfastly denied ever using biological weapons in combat. As a research scientist inside Fort Detrick, Dr. Olson probably knew the truth.

White House staff members Donald Rumsfeld and Richard Cheney promptly arranged for a meeting for the President to apologize to the family. They invited the family to the White House.

The Olsons withheld their lawsuit, accepted the invitation, and on July 21 met with President Gerald Ford. During a seventeen-minute meeting, Ford apologized and expressed sympathy on behalf of the American people. The family could look forward to some more financial compensation. Photos were taken as hands were shaken.

About a fortnight later, the family lunched at CIA headquarters as guests of Director William Colby. He did not reveal that, although Olson worked at the Fort Detrick US Army facility, Olson had actually been an employee of the CIA. Colby did give them copies of about 150 pages of CIA documents, with some parts redacted. And the CIA hoped that would end it.

The Olsons read it all, very carefully.

The Senate and the House Committees churned on, uncovering FBI and CIA wiretaps of public and antiwar figures and more details and reasons why the CIA needed to be held in check. The revelations about Frank Olson's death were not the main thrust of committee investigations. Gerald K. Haines, CIA historian, saw the hearings as "a power struggle between the legislative and executive branches in which Congress ... tried to regain control over US intelligence activities and foreign policy." The Committees asserted the rights of Congress and challenged White House reluctance to provide information. The White House argued to preserve their independent, separated power.

Congressman Pike suspected that what the CIA had been doing and what Olson's death implied was a story that no one wanted known. His House Select Committee on Intelligence pressed hard to see the CIA budgets and how tax money was used and for which purposes. He also sought Vietnam war records. The CIA resisted, knowing that beneath each number is something to be explained. Secretary of State Kissinger stonewalled the release of documents as unnecessary prying. Undaunted by the famous global power broker, Pike's committee issued Kissinger a citation of contempt.

At one point, President Ford instructed all administration officials to stop testifying and to stop providing documents. Then, after a tense week of closed-door negotiations, compromise was reached when Pike agreed that the President himself could retain the right to be the ultimate judge of what classified material could be released.

Over in the Senate, the Church Committee delved into the possible role of the CIA in the assassination of foreign leaders. They probed the Kennedy assassination. The public heard rumors that JFK's death was the result of a conspiracy involving organized crime, with involvement or advanced knowledge of the CIA and the FBI.

Recently, Antoinette Giancana, the daughter of crime boss Sam Giancana, asserted that her father and other important leaders did cooperate and were responsible for the killing of President Kennedy. The Committee did not get the chance to interrogate Sam Giancana because on June 19, 1975, the day before he was scheduled to testify, he was killed in his basement kitchen—by many small-caliber shots to the head. She suspects that CIA did it.

Crime member Johnny Roselli did testify on June 24. Jimmy Hoffa disappeared on July 30th. Johnny Roselli was killed a year later.

Even today, suspicion prevails that Oswald may well have been just a player in a bigger plan, as he himself said, a "patsy."

The Church Senate Committee Report concluded, "Secrecy is essential to covert operations; secrecy can, however, become a source of power, a barrier to serious policy debate within the government, and a means of circumventing the established checks and procedures of government. The Committee found that secrecy and compartmentalization contributed to a temptation on the part of the Executive to resort to covert operations in order to avoid bureaucratic, congressional, and public debate."

Congressman Pike was troubled by what the probes had discovered. William Blum, author of *Killing Hope*, at the 2003 Debate on Foreign Policy at Dublin, Ireland, reported that in an interview Pike had said of his committee's 1976 report that "not many (Congressmen) want to read it.... They think it is better not to know. There are too many things that embarrass Americans in that report.... They are asked to believe that this country has been evil. And nobody wants to believe that."

Senate and House committees agreed that the CIA should have more restrictions. Their Foreign Intelligence and Surveillance Act (FISA) of 1978 supported the idea of a permanent congressional intelligence committee. Clearly one intent was to keep better tabs on the Executive branch. Pike observed that "The CIA never did anything the White House didn't want. Sometimes they didn't want to do what they did."

Conservatives expressed concern that new constraints would slow down necessary policy actions. Senator John Stennis said, "If you are going to have an intelligence agency, you have to protect it as such…and shut your eyes some, and take what's coming."

In 2006, the CIA web site described its mission: "We are the eyes and ears of the nation and at times its hidden hand." It conducts "covert action at the direction of the President to preempt threats or achieve United States policy objectives." It believes "our success depends on our ability to act with total discretion and an ability to protect sources and methods."

Military personnel respect the chain of command. Military personnel are expected to obey orders. In civilian organizations, obedience comes with risk. If a boss tells a subordinate

"Take care of it. How you do it is up to you. Just do it and don't tell me how you did it," who is responsible if "doing it" is unethical or illegal? Does the subordinate have license to lie? Can the subordinate claim "he was just following orders," or has he no defense? Is the boss absolved of responsibility?

The 9/11 Commission observed that "committees headed by Frank Church...and Otis Pike...published evidence that the CIA had secretly planned to assassinate Fidel Castro and other foreign leaders. The President had not taken plain responsibility for these judgments. CIA officials had taken most of the blame, saying they had done so in order to preserve the President's 'plausible deniability.'"

Congressional committees had chilled the notion that US foreign policy could use assassination as a tool. This issue continued to float through the halls of Washington, undefined for years. President Jimmy Carter (1976-1980) affirmed the US disapproval of assassination. President Ronald Reagan brought it into focus. In his first year of office in 1981, he issued Executive Order #12333 which directed that "no employee of the United States government shall engage in or conspire to engage in political assassination." The order was silent on the issues of assassinating citizens or criminals without a trial and conviction.

Dr. Harold A. Abramson, then hunched over from his seventy-five years, was one of those who were glad the hearings were over. A summary of his recollections of his sessions with Olson in 1953 were in the record and had been given to the family. His name was in hearing records. His name was included in the *New York Times*. He had not been called to testify about the Olson case. He then sent a note to the author on his prescription pad, "Thank goodness DOD protects its own!"

If too many people know what is going on, the truth ultimately seeps out.

One particularly large CIA secret was too big to hide, even though the "Jennifer" project was managed by a company well practiced in keeping secrets. Back in March 1968, a Russian submarine with three nuclear weapon missiles aboard suffered explosions and sank. Neither the American nor Russian public knew the story. The CIA set out to try to retrieve the sub by building a special ship to do the job.

In 1974, on the Pacific Ocean north of Hawaii, was stationed a 618-foot long ship, the *Glomar Explorer*. Disinformation had described it as a specialized deep sea mining vessel intended to harvest manganese and other minerals from the ocean floor far below. The authorities in control were trying to make people believe it. However, too many people knew otherwise—those who designed it, those who built it, those who were its crew, those who brought supplies to it, and those who might want to brag how clever they were. The truth leaked out.

The cover was exposed in 1975 when the *Los Angeles Times* revealed that *Glomar Explorer* belonged to the Summa Corporation, the secretive company owned by secretive recluse Howard Hughes, and it was doing secret work. Later stories said the ship was grappling down 17,000 feet to retrieve an abandoned Russian submarine.

The Soviets had not known exactly where their submarine sank and they had no way to retrieve it. They surely guessed that the "mining vessel" was not grappling for minerals. The big ship secret was not a secret kept. How much was recovered or not *was* a secret kept. One disinformation story was that only some components had indeed been raised.

Modern day historian researchers, seeking more records about the project, tried exercising the Freedom of Information Act —only to evoke the response: "can neither confirm nor deny" whether records exist or not. This information barrier stands immutable when "classified information" is involved. The trusty phrase of evasion "No comment," now has a more elaborate companion: "can neither confirm nor deny." Either one says, in effect, "we won't tell you anything, not even a hint."

Nevertheless, after years of research here and in Russia, a detailed report has emerged. Most of the submarine was indeed recovered. Kenneth Sewell with Clint Richmond tell the fascinating tale in the book *Red Star Rogue—the Untold Story of a Submarine's Nuclear Strike Attempt on the U.S.*

Some notable changes in leadership were made during 1975. Ford appointed Rumsfeld as Secretary of Defense and elevated Cheney to Chief of White House Staff. And to show that there would be changes at the CIA, Ford accepted the retirement of DCI Colby and replaced him for 1976 with George Herbert Walker Bush, former Congressman from Texas and former Ambassador to the United Nations.

DCI Colby, shortly before leaving the CIA, signed a recommendation to pay the Olsons $1,250,000. One congressman apparently believed that was too generous and opined that those who do risky work know that there are risks. He prevailed and the amount was reduced. Congress approved a special settlement of $750,000. The family signed an agreement that claims against the government in the death of Frank Olson were thereby settled.

Ford ran for election in 1976 against Jimmy Carter, former governor of Georgia. Ford had a distinguished career in Congress and held the nation together after the Watergate scandal. But the media allowed the public to believe he was inept: he once hit a golf ball that hit another player, and on another occasion he stumbled on the steps of an airplane. Worst of all, he had pardoned Nixon. He lost to Jimmy Carter.

FDR
Truman
Eisenhower
Kennedy
Johnson
Nixon
Ford
Carter
Reagan

CHAPTER EIGHT

Iran, etc.

Anti-American hostility became ever more apparent during the next two decades. The United States desperately needed oil from the Middle East region. America used its economic and military muscle to openly (and covertly) act to protect US and allied interests, including survival for Israel.

Most Americans fancy themselves as good guys—saving the world from the Nazis in World War II, evicting invaders from South Korea, trying to preserve South Vietnam from communism, giving generously to needy peoples, paying a lion's share of the United Nations budgets.

It is discomforting to consider that America could be hated and despised. It is easier to deny it and ignore it.

A major and festering source of anti-American hostility was fueled by the United Nations decision of 1947 to partition Palestine into Arab and Jewish lands by carving out territory for a separate and independent state of Israel on May 4, 1948. Both Britain and the United States endorsed this action and committed themselves to supporting the survival of the new nation.

Palestinians protested and many Palestinians were expelled or sought refuge out of Israel and into nearby but less desirable lands. Sirhan Sirhan claimed attention for the refugee cause in 1968 by killing Senator Robert Kennedy. Then, at the Olympic games in Munich in September 1972, kidnappers seized nine Israeli athletes and demanded release of Palestinian prisoners in Israel. When their demands were rejected, they killed all nine athletes.

Egypt and Syria attacked Israel on Yom Kippur [Day of Atonement] in 1973. Israel retaliated with ferocity and seized Egyptian land. Fighting ended after eighteen days. Israel later withdrew from the Suez west bank. Eventually Egypt's President Anwar Sadat and Israel's Prime Minister Begin signed to end thirty years of conflict and set the stage for future return of Sinai land to Egypt.

More startling events would follow to assert rights for Palestinians and to spread Islam's influence in the world. The United States became a primary target.

Iranian fundamentalist Muslims had never accepted the regime of the Shah. In January 1979, in failing health, the Shah left Iran for medical treatment in the US and died in Egypt in July. The Ayatollah Khomeini, highly revered by Muslims, pronounced that the United States was "the great Satan." His fervent Islamic revolution followers stormed the United States embassy in Tehran and seized sixty-three US hostages. Weeks later, mobs in Libya attacked the US embassy there. In February, extremists shot and killed US Ambassador Adolph Dubs in Kabul, Afghanistan. A few months later, an American rescue raid, approved by President Jimmy Carter, fizzled in the desert.

Ronald Reagan campaigned for President in 1980. Just as he was taking office from Jimmy Carter in 1981, a formal accord obtained the release of the hostages in Iran.

Israeli aircraft destroyed a nuclear reactor in Iraq in June 1981. Palestinian supporters assassinated Egyptian President Anwar Sadat in October.

Then in September 1981, one Arab nation attacked another: Iraq intruded into Iran over disputed territory. Because Iran had taken Americans hostage in Tehran in 1979, the US was sympathetic to Iraq.

A truck bomb rolled to the US Marine headquarters at the Beirut airport in October 22, 1983. It exploded and killed 245 Marines and demolished much of the building. In addition, Hezbollah, a militant Shia group based in Lebanon believed to be supported by Iran, took some Americans as hostages.

At home, relations between the Reagan White House and Congress were severely strained by what became known as the Iran-Contra affair.

Like most earlier administrations, the Reagan executive branch of our government insisted that it, and not Congress, was in charge of foreign affairs. The notion of "separation of powers" was being tested by Reagan. Could Congress tell the President what to do and what not to do?

Congress cited the Constitution which says the "Powers of Congress include... To declare War.... To make Rules for the Government and Regulation of the land and naval Forces.... To make all Laws which shall be necessary and proper in carrying into Execution of the foregoing Powers, and all other Powers vested by the Constitution the Government of the United States, or in any Department or Officer thereof."

The US, through the CIA, an agency of the Executive Branch, had covertly supported the Contras in their fight to oust the socialist Sandanistas, who had taken control of Nicaragua in 1979. The Reagan administration, including Vice President George H. W. Bush, Secretary of State George Schultz, and CIA Director Bill Casey, wanted to continue that support. They were convinced that aiding the Contras was good for America.

Congress was concerned that involvement could escalate and enmesh the US in "another Vietnam." They blocked funds by means of the Boland Amendment. It banned the CIA, the Defense Department and any other government agency from any covert support of the Contras effective December 1983.

The White House wanted the Contras to succeed in Nicaragua and they wanted Hezbollah to release American hostages held in Lebanon.

In a complex, invisible deal, the National Security Council, not named in the ban, would arrange for Iran to buy hundreds of wire-guided missiles useful for its fight with Iraq and Iran would persuade Hezbollah to free the hostages. Iran would pay inflated prices. The excess "profit" would buy guns for the Contras. The administration planned to assert its independence of Congress and conduct foreign affairs without using US appropriations.

Coordinator of the project was Marine Corps Lt. Col. Oliver North, who had joined the National Security Council staff in 1981. The project was intentionally covert, using unconventional channels to deal, with sketchy records at best. It lacked the tight oversight and audit scrutiny of usual government projects. Iran got some antitank missiles, the Contras received some guns and funds, and Hezbollah released some hostages...and then took some more.

The story of this under-the-table deal finally leaked out in November 1986 when a Lebanese magazine reported that the White House had been flouting Congressional resolutions and was covertly running foreign policy off the books.

Democratic party leaders saw this as a chance to tarnish the image of the genial "teflon" president. Congressional Democrats charged that President Reagan bore full responsibility for any wrong doings. The White House could argue "plausible deniability": that Reagan was aloof from the project. President Reagan appointed former Senator John Tower to head a special commission to look into it. The Tower group pointed the finger at Defense Secretary Caspar Weinberger, National Security Advisor John Poindexter and Lt. Col. Oliver North. Formal charges were brought against them. They were tried and convicted.

Special Independent Counsel Lawrence Walsh concluded that the shipments of 1985 were illegal and violated a ban of sending military aid into Nicaragua and that the undocumented procedures opened opportunity for some people to commit monetary improprieties.

The administration was charged with withholding of relevant information from the Counsel. The administration was also charged with deliberately deceiving Congress and the public of the scope of these operations.

North's defenders said he had a job to do, he did it, and his superiors knew what he was doing. Ultimately, the convictions of North and Poindexter were overturned on appeal. Weinberger was pardoned by President George H.W. Bush.

Years later, the voters of Nicaragua elected Violet Chamorro as President and rejected the leadership of the Sandanistas.

In spite of his apparent knowledge of the plan and having admitted on national TV in 1987 that he made mistakes, President Reagan eluded all harpoons. Still open was the question of how to resolve an issue of separation of powers. Can the President ignore Congress? How shall the US adjudicate issues between the Presidency and the Congress? Back in 1975, President Ford and Congressman Pike had compromised their dispute. Reagan and Congress talked and postured until their conflict dissipated and the public, at least, no longer cared. Reagan's enemies dropped any plans to punish or impeach him—figuring that this elderly, popular gentleman would soon finish his second term and be out of office anyway.

Unanswered was the question as to what protection the public has from unscrutinized, unmonitored, off-the-books government ventures.

And while Washington's primary attention had been focused on Iran-Contra, a sporadic series of violent events began to capture public attention.

CHAPTER NINE

Anger

Each occasional terrorist act over the years seemed isolated or unconnected to others. One was PLO, one was by Abu Nidal, one was Libya, one was Al Qaeda, one was Hamas, one was rumored to be Iran, or one Iraq, etc. Americans did not see that overall it was a fabric, loosely woven, but with a common thread and a big design: oust Israel, oust the USA, disrupt the West and its economic power, escalate the pain, spread Islam. The terrorists were predominantly Arabic. They were extremist Muslims—fundamentalist in faith and extreme in their actions. They resented us and envied our prosperity and our privileges. They disapproved of our indulgent lifestyle and of women's freedom. Usama bin Laden's strategist deputy, Ayman al Zawahiri, in 1998 urged every Muslim who could, in any country, "Kill the Americans and their allies."

Our leadership and our media failed to make this larger pattern understood. The public had been upset by "militants," or "terrorists," or the "insurgents," or the "extremists." It is a war, a new kind of war. Terrorism is not itself the enemy. It is a method. There is no geographic focal point which we could destroy or bomb. The terrorist is not a random person—he is an anti-American. It is the anti-American who is the enemy of America.

As self-proclaimed guardians of world culture, the major media is especially tolerant of any non-Western religion. As a result, we were poorly informed about the unity of the undercurrent of hostility aimed at our way of life.

We need to buy Arab oil and we need the uninterrupted flow of oil. We need to be able to work with their governments and leadership to assure that oil still flows. Many of the nations in the Middle East want cleric government, to integrate religion into all aspects of society and government. An elected representative government is antithetical to an Islamic theocracy. They resist our pushing for an elected structure, our ideas of a democratic republic.

Extremist Islam is a belief system, not a nation state. Those most dedicated to ousting the US from the Middle East, causing our downfall and eliminating Israel, are not necessarily a recognized "nation." "Terrorist" groups are scattered, elusive, and—other than al Qaeda—without a famous leader like Usama bin Laden. Their operational home bases are temporary and hidden. They do share some common goals and objectives, but often have differing strong, religious, factional loyalties. If they were to convene simultaneously, there likely would be some conflict as to who should be the leader of a unified movement. "They" are not fully united among/between themselves. And even within the region, there can be conflict between Iraq's Sunnis and Shiites. But Muslims do seem to be virtually unanimous about wanting the nation of Israel to be gone and Israeli land to be returned to Arabs.

The extremist Taliban group still seeks control of Afghanistan and has provided shelter for elusive al Qaeda which has no city seat of government. Al Qaeda is perhaps the most fervent enemy of the US, Britain—and even of Arabic Saudi Arabia. Moderate or cooperative Arabic nations are cautious themselves: Egypt, Jordan, Pakistan, UAE, Kuwait. Most openly anti-US governments are Iran, Libya, Syria, and Palestine.

During the last 30 years, the anti-American groups have used terrorist tactics—on the ground, at sea, and in the air—to disrupt and to gain concessions or to force retreat. Fundamentalist Muslims want a system where personal, daily life, social and governing systems are unified, guided by principles in the Koran. Their devotion to their religion and to their state are the same. Those who undermine Islam, attack or support attacks on Islamic nations, are serious enemies. Devout Muslims are willing to give their lives for Islam. Persons who abandon Islam are, in essence, traitors and, as in may societies, face the penalty for treason—death.

Leaders in Britain, Australia, and the United States, though severely criticized by those who want peace now, have stood firm—and have consistently insisted that "we will not yield to terrorism." Nonetheless, western nations have been generally reluctant to see the long-term nature of the terrorist conflict and just want the violence to end.

Gradually, more Americans were becoming more clear about who was the enemy. Attacks escalated.

Six men seized control of the cruise liner, *Achille Lauro*, off Egypt in October of 1985 and demanded the release of fifty Palestinians held in Israeli prisons. When their demand was rejected, they shot an elderly Jewish American in his wheel chair and threw him overboard to die. They only left the ship after being provided with a special airliner to fly them to Egypt. But then US Navy jets forced that airliner to land in

Italy where the hijackers were captured. The terrorist leader died of natural causes in US custody in Iraq in 2004.

Palestinian terrorists hijacked a TWA Flight 847 at Beirut for seventeen days in 1985, demanding that Israel release some Shiite prisoners.

May 17, 1987 an Iraqi missile hit the *USS Stark* in the Persian Gulf and killed thirty-seven aboard. Iraq said it was a mistake and apologized.

In 1987, relations with Russia softened up, in spite of the United States having provided Stinger missiles which were so devastatingly effective against Russian helicopters in Afghanistan. Premier Gorbachev and President Reagan agreed to dismantle thousands of ground-to-ground attack missiles.

During the eight years of the Iraq-Iran War, United States sentiments swayed one way and the other. Hundreds of thousands of lives on both sides were destroyed before the war concluded in 1988. Iraqi, Persian and US relations were chilly at best.

US-Iran relations tensed up again in July 1988. The US guided missile cruiser *Vincennes*, armed with the advanced Aegis system, was cruising in the Persian Gulf when radar detected a jet approaching from Iran. Believing itself under attack, *Vincennes* shot the plane down with a surface-to-air missile. It was a tragic error. The jet was a passenger airliner, Iran Air Flight 655. All 290 people aboard died.

Civilian airliners had not been invulnerable to military action. Russian fighter planes shot down a South Korean airliner in 1983 when it strayed over soviet airspace. Some 269 people died. In spite of these shootdowns, no airline was deterred from continuing normal operations.

PanAm jumbo airliner, Flight 103, flying over Lockerbie, Scotland, and heading for the United States, blew up when a bomb in a suitcase exploded. All 289 on board and eleven people on the ground died on December 28, 1988. Prolonged tedious analysis of fragment clues finally led to the conviction of a former Libyan intelligence agent. Fifteen years later, in 2003, the Libyan government accepted responsibility and began paying compensation to victim families.

The USSR had been bent upon ruling Afghanistan, but the Afghans resisted tenaciously. The United States sent almost 1,000 Stinger shoulder-launched anti-aircraft missiles to the Mujahadeen in 1986-87. The early Stingers weighed about 35 pounds and could easily fly five miles and reach altitudes of 10,000 feet. After losing hundreds of its aircraft to Stinger missiles, Russia finally withdrew in 1989 and left Soviet puppet administrators in charge. They were later usurped by the Taliban in 1996. The Mujahadeen then directed their energies against the Islamic fundamentalist Taliban, with support from the United States. Some of the Stinger missiles had found their way into the hands of Mujahadeen allies and some Stingers were acquired on the black market. More than one civilian aircraft was reportedly brought down by a Stinger. In spite of CIA efforts to repurchase them, dozens of deadly Stingers were in anti-US hands.

Iraq had long coveted the oil-rich lands of Kuwait. In 1990, Iraqi military forces of President Saddam Hussein surged into the relatively defenseless nation. The United States marshaled aircraft, tanks and troops and missile-carrying ships and then overwhelmingly attacked the Iraqi forces in Kuwait and government offices in Baghdad. Iraqi forces were crushed and expelled from Kuwait in a matter of weeks. It cost the US 148 dead. President George H. Bush stopped the war at the Iraq border, though critics thought we should have pressed all the way to Baghdad and taken Hussein.

This was the first time the United States used long-range cruise missiles in battle. These "stand off" weapons allow the shooter to reach hundreds of miles into enemy territory while laying back a safe distance. Unlike ballistic missiles which arch high up and then come crashing down, cruise missiles reach their far-away targets while flying close the ground, below radar detection, at the subsonic speed of a fast jet airplane. The Navy's twenty-foot-long Tomahawk had been in development for decades and was launched from both surface ships and submarines with great effectiveness in the Persian Gulf War.

Iraqi defenses were unable to down significant numbers of the incoming Tomahawks. They came in low. They came in fast. They flew confusing zigzag routes. The defenders were hard put to shoot them down. The United States saw how difficult it was for Iraq to defend against cruise missiles and began developing means to defend the United States from such missiles. In the works, in both the United States and the Soviet Union, were cruise missiles which would fly at supersonic speeds and which would be even harder to shoot down.

TV captured the Kuwait Gulf War—or Desert Storm as it was named—in real time. The public had never been so close to war action. Americans were proud of the overwhelming victory. Meanwhile, quietly, the Olson case was below the media radar.

In February of 1993, Ramzi Ahmed Yousef masterminded a plot to use a truck loaded with explosives to bring down the World Trade Center in New York City. He succeeded in getting the vehicle into a below-ground parking garage where it exploded. Six people died, but the building survived. The public had no sense of what this attack symbolized nor what it might portend.

The next year, while on the run, Yousef and his uncle, Khalid Sheikh Mohammed, a subordinate of al Qaeda leader Usama bin Laden, began planning to put bombs on and blow up US jumbo airliners over the Pacific as a way to punish the United States for supporting Israel. They did this scheming while in Manila. Authorities had been tracking Yousef and finally caught and arrested him the next year in Pakistan.

In 1996, President Bill Clinton, a genial man who enjoyed a positive media image, had been looking ahead to run for a second term. The Democratic Convention was coming up in August and the election would be in November. There was reason for optimism. The Nation would host the International Olympics, to open in August in Atlanta. The United States mood was good. But then a personal disappointment, in early summer.

Clinton learned that Arkansas friend Governor Jimmy Guy Tucker had been convicted of conspiracy, and business associates Jim and Susan McDougal convicted of fraud.

In June, an explosion far away disrupted the feeling of good will.

An attack was directed at the US military in the Khobar Towers housing complex in Saudi Arabia. A bomb exploded, killing nineteen American servicemen. The Saudis seized some suspects. The US government criticized a US general for inadequate safety precautions.

Ramzi Ahmed Yousef was finally put on trial in New York. The *New York Times* reported on July 10 that Yousef and others had once planned to blow up twelve airliners. At least he was now in custody.

But just one week later a TWA Boeing 747, as Flight TWA 800, took off from New York headed for Paris and blew up only fifteen minutes after takeoff. Washington immediately assumed that TWA was a victim of terrorism by either a bomb or possibly a shoulder-launched Stinger missile.

Initially denied, but later admitted, was the fact that a variety of military equipment—submarines, surface craft, an Aegis type naval missile cruiser, vessels of a number of US allies, and some smaller, fast craft—were positioned at that time for defensive exercises in the Atlantic from Massachusetts down past New York and further south.

CHAPTER TEN

Tale of Two Sparks

At 8:31 P.M. on Wednesday, July 17, 1996, in clear skies above the Atlantic Ocean off of Long Island, shortly after takeoff from New York's Kennedy Airport and bound for Paris, TWA Flight 800 was at 13,700 feet when it exploded. All 230 people aboard the Boeing 747 died. Hundreds of people in boats, planes, and on the shore watched the horror of the broken plane and flaming fuel and debris falling into the Atlantic Ocean. Initial radio and TV stories reported that scores of witnesses had seen what might have been one or more missiles rising up and shooting the airplane down.

Analysts remembered that eight years earlier, on July 3, 1988, a US Navy missile cruiser, the *Vincennes*, situated by the Strait of Hormuz of the Arabian Gulf, mistook an approaching Iranian A-300 Airbus airliner to be a hostile Iranian jet fighter. The cruiser launched a missile which brought down the Airbus causing the death of all 290 on board.

Speculation began: could it have happened again? Rumors reached the Clinton White House that a Navy missile did it. Almost immediately after the disaster, the highest levels in the Federal government announced that a missile did it, and that it was probably a terrorist or criminal action. Some speculated that it was revenge for the Hormuz shoot-down. Former National Security Advisor Anthony Lake recalled on "CNN Presents" in 2006 that the administration suspected terrorism and "wanted to look for an Iranian connection." In just a few days, the Summer Olympics were to begin in Atlanta. The international good will was now chilled by fear of possible US retaliation.

Normally, air crash investigations are the responsibility of the National Transportation Safety Board (NTSB). However, in this case a criminal act was suspected, so the Federal Bureau of Investigation (FBI) had primary jurisdiction to lead the investigation. New York area boss of the FBI, James Kallstrom, would direct the probe. A Marine veteran of Vietnam, Kallstrom, 53, took charge with skills honed by twenty-five years of investigative experience. In Paris, the Surete (French National Police) also investigated the tragedy.

Eventually, more than 100 documented witnesses at different vantage points reported seeing a streak or streaks heading toward the plane prior to the explosion. Extracts from their comments include these: "flame rising from the ocean," "big streak of light moving vertically," "fire arching upward with a smoke trail," "rising up, going toward the plane...two objects."

The witnesses included Paul Angelides, a court-certified engineer, on the shore; sailors on boats; Dwight Brumley, a retired Navy Master Chief, aboard an airplane; and Maj. Frederick Meyer, a Vietnam veteran pilot and his copilot, in a helicopter which was first to reach the scene.

Attention concentrated on small, easily-launched missiles such as the Stingers which had been so effective when used by Afghan fighters against Russian planes and helicopters. The FBI circulated photographs of Stinger containers and Stinger-type launch tubes and encouraged boat-people and shoreline people who might find such evidence to come forward. The FBI began interviewing hundreds of witnesses who had seen something on that clear July evening.

Much of the nose section of the fuselage had been blown off, and then the plane broke up, tanks ruptured and fuel burned. Debris was scattered and sunk over a large area. Investigators needed to retrieve the cockpit voice recorder and the flight data recorder from the wreckage to gain clues to what happened.

The FBI directed recovery of the bodies and wreckage from a wide area of the sea and on the bottom. Pieces were brought to a huge aircraft factory hanger at the former Grumman Corporation facility at Calverton, New York. There, the giant 747 was "reconstructed" and examined for clues. At least one of the retrieved pieces of significant size reportedly turned up missing. This piece would later be the subject of a lawsuit.

Although capable commercial vessels with divers were in the area, retrieval of the recorders was delayed until government ships could arrive with Navy Special Weapons Team personnel to dive down to retrieve the recorder boxes.

The recorders were found and then were sent to the lab of the manufacturer for transcribing and analyzing the data. The recordings attested that the flight crew had no warning.

During the early phases of the investigation, the FBI withheld from the NTSB access to 244 witness interview reports. This delay, or "wall," seemed deliberately slow and inhibited the NTSB's work.

Days before the late August 1996 Democratic National Convention, official policy veered away from the missile theory. Washington shifted position: it was not a missile. Concerns about fears of military confrontations abated.

Retired but well-known newsman Pierre Salinger stirred up controversy. But not wanting to disrupt the election process he waited until two days after the reelection of President Bill Clinton. Salinger, 71, who had been press secretary for Presidents Kennedy and Johnson, then announced that the government was covering up the truth of TWA 800. The plane was, he said, a victim of "friendly fire." He said a French intelligence agent gave him a document—later identified as e-mail that had been circulating for months—coming from the Internet "written by a secret service agent." Almost immediately untraceable rumors spread questioning Salinger's credibility.

FBI's Kallstrom discounted the document as nonsense. On CNN, the investigation director said, "The United States military did not shoot a missile at this airplane. The United States military did not shoot anything." He said that the jet was brought down either by a bomb, a missile, or a mechanical malfunction. But if it was a missile, Kallstrom said it was not fired by the United States.

In "The Counter Terrorist" article in a 2002 *New Yorker* magazine, author Lawrence Wright reported on a White House meeting early on with Richard Clarke, the US counterterrorism czar. Clarke recalled that John O'Neill, a key terrorist investigator of the FBI, had concluded that the range of a Stinger was too short to reach up to the TWA 800.

If an enemy wanted to use a shoulder-launched Stinger-type missile to hit an airliner, he would have a better shot at it if his ambush were nearer to JFK airport where planes would be lower and more reachable.

O'Neill suggested the possibility that what witnesses saw as streaks was merely burning fuel as the headless plane climbed. The CIA would consider the case for an on-board explosion and construct a computer animation showing the airplane zooming upward, after the nose blew off, trailing burning fuel as it climbed. The missile idea was ruled out even though more than 100 witnesses were certain that one or more missiles caused the disaster.

Then in January 1997, before the FBI had completed its work, word leaked out that the Alcohol, Tobacco and Firearms Department (ATF) of the US Treasury Department had concluded that the explosion was not caused by sabotage or a missile, but was the result of a mechanical malfunction of some kind. Kallstrom protested that the FBI wasn't done yet and that the ATF report was premature. But the government focus shifted away from a missile as a cause.

Woe be to someone who has evidence which the government owns. James Sanders, a journalist and former police investigator, and his wife, Elizabeth, were prosecuted for illegal possession of evidence—pieces of seat upholstery given to the Sanders by an airline pilot acquaintance who was part of the team reassembling the TWA 800 airplane at Calverton.

This pilot friend of the Sanders believed that some strange reddish material on one row of seats might be residue from a missile explosive and therefore merited lab analysis. When leaders of the reconstruction project chose not to do that, this friend snipped two small samples of the fabric and gave them to Mrs. Sanders. The Sanders in turn engaged an independent lab to analyze the chemical composition of the reddish stuff. The tests discovered substances which could conceivably be components from a rocket propellant. The FBI argued that it was merely part of glue from the upholstery process.

The Sanders were tried and convicted in Federal Eastern District Court in Uniondale, New York, but when sentenced they received probation and were released. James Sanders told their story in *Altered Evidence*. The pilot friend was not prosecuted in exchange for identifying the Sanders.

Pierre Salinger was subdued until a CNN interview in March 1997, when he and former ABC newsman Mike Somner cited radar information—and hypothesized that a defense missile meant to hit a "Tomahawk Missile" had "lost its lock." The FBI seized from still another former pilot, Richard Russell, a tape of FAA radar images, said to be the basis for Salinger's statements. By spring, Salinger apologized to the US Navy, but he would not retreat from the idea that a missile did it.

Many months later the official verdict was finally issued by the NTSB: TWA 800 came apart because vapors in the center fuel tank were ignited to explode by a stray spark from possibly frayed wiring.

Reed Irvine, head of the independent organization Accuracy in Media, charged the Clinton Administration with conspiring to cover up the facts of a shoot-down by a missile.

For seasoned Boeing 747 pilots, the official verdict seemed unlikely. One reason they doubted that a small spark set off fuel vapors is an event that had occurred a year earlier involving the very same airplane. This involved a spark—a giant, giant spark: lightning. Airliners are struck by lightning more often than passengers would like to know. Albert Mundo, an experienced 747 engineer, was on that flight and recalled what happened. The airplane was approaching Rome on Good Friday morning in April of 1995 when the lightning struck.

Lightning strikes involve extraordinarily high voltages and current flows in the thousands of amperes. Lightning struck this airplane on the right wing tip, transversed through the plane, and then out the other side. A few minutes later it was hit again. The mighty plane shuddered again, but continued on and landed normally at Rome. Missing or badly burned by intense heat were parts of the wing tip. Twenty-five square feet of structure had to be replaced. It is significant that at the time of the lightning strike the amount of fuel in the center wing tank was almost identical to the amount of fuel in the tank in the TWA 800 case. It is also significant that the airplane was at about the same altitude and ambient air temperature as TWA 800. One wonders how a small spark in the airplane could ignite the center fuel tank when thousands and thousands of amperes had raced through that same airplane without an explosion.

And the upward zoom climb with a blunt fuselage? Another veteran 747 captain, Ray Lahr, showed that such dynamic behavior was inconsistent with physics and aerodynamic principles. He sought access to the CIA analysis to challenge their hypothesis. The agency resisted revealing its calculations. His suit for Freedom of Information is still clogged in a legal mill.

Grumman test pilot Corky Meyer knows how a plane behaves if it suddenly loses its streamline nose: it quickly slows down, as if the brakes were applied, and starts to fall. Meyer was testing an F9F fighter jet in 1951 when the nose blew off. The plane slowed, shuddered and began to stall. Only with full throttle and sharp descent did Meyer avoid the stall and bring the limping jet to the nearest airport.

Plane maker Boeing normally defends its reputation fiercely as a builder of safe aircraft. Boeing made no defensive statement to the conclusion that a small spark set off tank vapors and instead indicated that it would respect the NTSB findings. Families of TWA 800 victims filed suits for damages. A special court procedure was established to encourage early submission of claims so that claimants could have their settlements quickly. Boeing was essentially passive, and instead of litigation dragging out for years, the TWA 800 claims were settled surprisingly quickly.

Perhaps Boeing believed that quick court resolution would be more considerate of distraught families and less costly than if they fought the official verdict. Cynics could opine that by being a gracious loser in this case, Boeing might preserve its good government relations and thereby enhance their chances of Export-Import Bank financing of airliner sales and winning favorable military contracts for some of its other products such as its F-18 fighters or its air tankers.

The FBI suspended its search for a criminal cause in November 1997, and a month later James Kallstrom retired from the FBI.

He joined MBNA Bank as a Senior Executive Vice President. Just after 9/11 in 2001, Governor George Pataki asked him to be his advisor as head of the Office of Public Security for the State of New York. Kallstrom took leave from the bank to serve, unpaid.

Meanwhile, independent researchers were also analyzing radar data and interviewing witnesses, many of whose sightings reinforced the idea that a missile or two missiles brought TWA 800 down.

Federal Aviation Administration radar records showed hundreds of boats and planes in the area for miles around the disaster. Government analysts were able to identify each one. Except one vessel.

Immediately after the explosions, all surface craft moved toward the scene to see what happened or to offer help to any survivors. Except one. This unidentified blip, a boat or ship, was almost directly below TWA 800 at the instant, but then left the scene at the extraordinary speed of 30 knots or more. When the FBI was asked what was this blip, the answer was "probably a helicopter." Could this mysterious surface craft have launched missiles which brought down TWA 800?

Was this blip, or craft, one of ours? An ally? Or some attacker?

On that fateful day in 1996, the world had been looking forward to the upcoming summer Olympics at Atlanta, Georgia. Because of the murderous attacks on Israeli athletes in Munich of 1972, all Olympic Games since have been provided with extraordinary security precautions. Land, sea, and air forces were on the alert. Radars were watching. Satellites were watching.

Defense training exercises in the Atlantic coastal region often go on.

CHAPTER ELEVEN

No Whistle

Part of a defense training exercise could have been to test our ability to intercept an incoming cruise missile or aircraft flying below the radar. A target drone could be sent to penetrate the area and simulate a low-flying aircraft or hostile Tomahawk-type cruise missile. The defenders would track and be ready to destroy it, using gunfire, air-to-air missiles or surface-to-air missiles. A drone is good for target practice. Defenders can also "shoot" at it with cameras or radar and "hits" are recorded. A drone could pass through the target area physically unscathed and cruise on out to fall into the sea and be recovered. Or the shoots and hits could be real. A drone has no warhead, but can have some explosive which can be commanded to self destruct if it strays toward something it shouldn't.

In the area that July night were a submarine, ocean surface craft, and, overhead, a Navy P3V patrol plane. These military assets would be mindful of the proximity to fishermen, pleasure boaters, and Long Island itself.

The pretend cruise missile may have been released from a mother airplane or boost-launched off a submarine or surface ship. Subsonic drones had been useful exercise targets for years. Even a few supersonic drones, bought from Russia, had been evaluated by our Navy.

Military warning zones, printed on airways maps, at times can be "activated" and require that private and commercial aircraft must fly high above them. On this tragic July evening, the incident occurred near a zone which was "active." However, because of heavy air traffic, the TWA 800 airplane was directed to delay its normal ever-climbing flight path and instead pass at 13,800 feet.

Now here is one theory of how a missile might have downed TWA 800. There are probably many other theories. Down below the airliner's path, the drone approached the defense forces. The surface ships were ready to shoot it down. As the drone crossed into their target area, this large airplane, TWA 800, unexpectedly intruded across the stage (though at a higher altitude). The defenders fired a missile or missiles at the drone. But then the missile-homing sensors saw instead a much larger, more pronounced target and homed in on it, the airliner. The missile or missiles went on up and exploded near or into TWA 800, blowing off much of its fuselage nose section and leading to breakup of the plane and the subsequent giant fuel-air explosion.

It may even be conceivable that the drone itself strayed towards the airliner and the defenders fired surface-to-air missiles to try to stop it. Concerned that the missiles wouldn't make it in time, the defenders actuated the drone's destruct explosive, but too late and too close, and it caused fatal damage to TWA.

Perhaps the missiles that did bring down TWA 800 could have been launched automatically by an allied vessel or by a hostile surface craft. So what about the mystery ship which raced away from under the scene of the disaster?

There are fast, 35-knot, ships that are tall enough to be seen over the horizon by shore-based radar. One class that comes to mind is the swift Patrol Coastal Ship designed by Vosper Thorneycroft of Britain, in service with allies, and the US derivative, the Cyclone Class, of which fourteen were built. The Navy's Cyclone-type supported Naval Special Warfare personnel and carry armament that could include not only guns but Stinger missiles. (A few years after TWA 800, some of the versatile Cyclones were transferred to the Coast Guard, but later reclaimed by the Navy.)

Why could we identify every radar blip except the runaway ship/boat? Was it racing away to retrieve a drone? Was it a perpetrator? If it had been the missile launcher, why did we not capture or sink it? If it did no wrong, why has it not been identified? Did we not chase it because we knew who or what it was? Michael Rivero, who often posts insightful commentaries on the Internet, likened this to the Sherlock Holmes tale of the dog that did not bark.

The highest levels of our government could have decided early that the national interest would be best served by diverting attention from the true cause of the explosion.

There may have been an overwhelming reason, or perhaps a combination of reasons, to cover up the facts. Those in authority remembered the almost panic caused by the Cuban Missile Crisis of 1962. A national election was coming up in November. The White House may have believed that admitting that a missile did it could:

1. lead to accusations and a confrontation which would threaten world peace;

2. disrupt the good will surrounding the world's Olympic Games;

3. shatter traveler confidence in air travel and dampen US prosperity;

4. expose secrets or weaknesses of US and allied security forces and weaken public confidence in government; or

5. inject unpredictable issues into the presidential election campaign.

These concerns echo the policies of Prime Minister Neville Chamberlain of the 1930's as the Nazis tested Britain's strength and will: peace at any price.

Missiles were ruled out.

The public was well aware of the missiles possibility. Controversy could be expected. Only the highest level could make the choice and then make it stick.

A plausible explanation was selected which, on its own merits, would do no harm and which would enhance aviation safety anyway. The tragedy of TWA 800 could be cause to improve airline safety. After designating a spark as the cause of the disaster, the NTSB mandated aircraft system changes to reduce the chances of explosive ignition of fuel vapors in partly empty tanks. These changes would increase the cost of the airplanes, but could add an additional safety factor. The selection reassured America that air travel would be getting safer. Ironically, ten years after the disaster, the FAA had not implemented the new requirement, apparently not convinced of crucial urgency.

The official verdict implies that there was neither terrorist attack nor friendly fire. Challenging that, Dr. Thomas Stalcup, Chairman of Flight 800 Independent Researchers Organization (FIRO), said that,

> *FIRO believes that the probable cause for the crash of TWA Flight 800 was an explosion caused by an external ignition source. Radar data, forensic analyses, debris field evidence, secret government test results, and multiple eyewitness observations all suggest that the external ignition source was most likely a surface-to-air missile.*

According to unreleased NTSB Exhibit 4A, more than 100 witnesses saw what looked like a missile (or missiles). What had they seen? In spite of compelling reports from whose who saw the streak(s), the FBI discounted them. Investigator Kallstrom explained that in legal procedures "eyewitness testimony is not evidence." This rule may have been inspiration for comedian Groucho Marx to quip, "Are you going to believe me or your lying eyes!"

On CNN, Kallstrom had said if a missile did strike the plane, it was not fired by the US. Whose missile was it? Kevin Ready and Cap Parlier, in their well documented book, *TWA 800: Accident or Incident*, proposed in 1998 that "there is sufficient reason to believe a terrorist act, quite probably perpetrated by the Government of Iran and/or its coconspirators, was committed upon TWA 800."

Perhaps an insider will conclude that there has been illegal behavior and will come forward and "blow the whistle."

Only a very brave person dares to blow the whistle on his boss. When he does, he faces retaliation, loss of career, and/or loss of respect as the organization starts rumors about his credibility or very sanity. A member of organized crime knows that a whistle blower is a "rat" who faces summary execution.

Congress enacted the first Whistle Blower Protection Act in 1989. It was intended to protect from reprisal people who call attention to illegal activity of their superiors.

A few TWA 800 government investigators may have had serious reservations but were reluctant to speak out, for fear of looking foolish, endangering National Security or facing retribution or prosecution. The truth was buried under the protective regulations of National Security.

Interestingly enough, while the TWA 800 investigation was underway, the Whistle Blower Protection Act lost some of its effectiveness. President Clinton issued Executive Order #13039, which withdrew whistle blower protection for members of the Naval Special Warfare group. Some TWA researchers suspect that this was to prevent any news leaks about any special airplane fragments found or details about what the data recorders might have revealed. Penalty for military personnel disobeying orders can be overwhelming and may be considered treasonous.

Truth can be suppressed by classifying a subject as a "Matter of National Security." And courts can seal records out of consideration for living persons. This course could be temporary or limited for some years. For example, sensitive personal family information gathered during the Kennedy assassination investigation were to be sealed for decades. After enough time, the truth about the TWA 800 accident and coverup will emerge. Some TWA 800 facts were being held by the FBI on the basis that the investigation was not actually closed.

Those who did not have the facts or authorization to know the truth have been deflected, blocked from access to important facts, or dare not risk prosecution for prying too deeply.

The spark verdict for TWA 800 blatantly ignores the preponderance of eyewitness observations. The findings reject objective interpretation of data. The credibility of government has deteriorated.

If it was a mistake by an ally or our own military, the truth has been obfuscated.

If it was terrorism, we should have been alerted so we could be better prepared for aviation attacks. If it was done by an enemy, what may have started as a coverup story—to buy time as we readied a response—stretched on, and on—and became irrevocable. The enemy found that we don't hit back.

A number of people who probably knew the truth of TWA 800 have died. Gone is Admiral Tom Moorer. Gone is Pierre Salinger. Gone is Commander Bill Donaldson. Gone is Reed Irvine.

History will determine if the nation was a winner because of the decision to cover up or deflect the truth.

Admiral Moorer, a former Chairman of the US Joint Chiefs of Staff, long suspected that a missile brought down TWA 800. At a Flight 800 Independent Researchers Organization

(FIRO) conference in 1999, the retired admiral said that the final story would remain elusive until a congressional hearing compels government officials to testify. Congressional action or otherwise, the truth will ultimately be known.

At the request of the author in 2001, Congressman Virgil Goode relayed to the cognizant Congressional Committees these requests:

1. The House Transportation Committee, Subcommittee on Aviation: hold hearings to listen to eyewitnesses who saw the disaster.

2. The House Judiciary Committee, Subcommittee on the Constitution: explore the validity of NTSB conclusions in the context of delayed and/or incomplete access to relevant facts.

Neither committee took up the requests.

CHAPTER TWELVE

Who Knew

September eleventh, 9/11. Seared in our minds, shown and re-shown on TV, the attack and collapse of the World Trade Center. Crash into the Pentagon. Crash in Pennsylvania. More killed than at Pearl Harbor. Horrible. Unforgettable.

Nineteen young Middle Eastern men, ready to sacrifice their own lives, hijacked four airliners and attacked the United States homeland and killed 2,973 people in airliners and on the ground, damaged the Pentagon, and destroyed the enormous twin towers of the World Trade Center (WTC) all within seventy-six minutes on the morning of September 11, 2001. Some 343 of those killed included fire, rescue and police personnel, as well as FBI terrorist expert John O'Neill.

On that morning, the symbol of western world prominence was brought down. The symbol of American military power was damaged. The symbol of American government barely escaped when one plane crashed in Pennsylvania. And America's sense of security would never be the same again.

Five of the men were passengers on American Airlines Flight 11, a Boeing 767, which left Boston's Logan Airport at 7:59 a.m., headed for Los Angeles. They hijacked the plane and crashed it into the North Tower of the WTC forty-seven minutes after takeoff.

Another group of four of the men, also at Logan, boarded United Airlines 175, also a Boeing 767, which left for Los Angeles as 8:14. They hijacked it and crashed it into the South Tower of the WTC at 9:03, just seventeen minutes after the North Tower had been hit.

Another group of five men boarded American Airlines Flight 77, a Boeing 757, at Washington's Dulles Airport which left for Los Angeles at 8:20. The hijackers crashed it into a side of the Pentagon at 9:37.

The last of the group, four men, were passengers at Newark Airport on United Airlines Flight 99, which left for San Francisco at 8:42. Believed to be targeted for either the White House or the Capitol, this flight crashed in Shanksville, Pennsylvania at 10:03 after a struggle between passengers and the hijackers.

Rumors said it was shot down. There was a bang. A piece of the plane and a few luggage items fluttered down to the ground eight miles from where Flight 99 crashed. After learning of the WTC hits, the White House authorized a possible shoot down as the plane seemed headed to Washington, probably for the Capitol or the White House.

Because of chaos within it, Flight 99 was flying in a chaotic way and could well have crashed where it did anyway. It was flying at a speed of 400-500 mph and would have flown six or eight miles in one minute. The piece(s) could have separated because of an on-board explosion, because of a cannon or missile hit, or because of structural failure from over-rigorous maneuvering during the fight in the cockpit. There will be more analysis, research and interpretation. Whether shot down or not, the passengers behaved heroically.

Americans were shocked. Horrified. Angry. Frustrated by the realization that we couldn't seize the perpetrators and try them, convict and punish them. A primary purpose of the United States government is to "provide for the common defense." It failed to do that on 9/11/01. This is somebody's fault.

How could this happen? Why couldn't we have prevented it? Why did President George W. Bush keep reading to school children in a Florida classroom? Who knew about it and when did they know?

The coordinated attack was the result of meticulous planning and preparation begun more than a year earlier. The idea itself may have been brewing for years. Each team needed at least one man who knew the basics of an airliner's controls, operating the radio, navigating to the chosen target, and guiding it up or down. There would be no need to know how to make a landing, smooth or otherwise. He would have had some basic flight instruction.

The plotters analyzed airline schedules to orchestrate a simultaneous, multi-prong attack. Winter, with its unpredictable weather, was ruled out. Midsummer afternoons, with thunderstorms that can disrupt flights, were ruled out. Morning take-offs were preferred when departures are most often on time.

They would have practiced being passengers in the specific kinds of airplanes and known about airport screening and boarding procedures for each airline and airport. The perpetrators were scattered and only directed to convene at the last moment.

The attackers had been patient, deliberate, thorough and secretive. They knew that secrecy was essential for their plan. They kept their secrets well.

There had long been rumors and suspicions that al Qaeda and followers of Usama Bin Laden intended to strike hard at America's homeland. Attacks were expected. But no one seemed to know exactly where, exactly how, and exactly when. Surely our intelligence organizations had real clues. If our government did not know that this was about to happen, why not? Don't we have moles, tipsters, agents, or friends who keep us informed?

If someone in our government did indeed know in advance, how is it that the word did not get to those who could prevent it or defend against it?

The United States government intelligence community included the Central Intelligence Agency (CIA), the National Security Agency (NSA), the Federal Bureau of Investigation (FBI), the Defense Intelligence Agency (DIA) of the Defense Department, as well as intelligence groups in the State Department, the Army, The Navy, Air Force, Marines, Coast Guard, Treasury Department, and the Department of Energy. These groups could also avail themselves of information from the wire services, media news organizations, and private businesses at home and abroad. Internet logs and message boards overflow with chatter and, maybe, important clues. Somewhere was information, obvious or not, that might have been the key warning of the 9/11 disaster.

America was and still is awash with information and analyses. Within the tidal waves of reports, rumors, bits and tips are some crucial facts. Decision makers need to know which ones. The challenge is to digest and assemble the puzzle pieces into a meaningful picture.

The President and the Congress created the National Commission on Terrorist Attacks Upon the United States to determine how it happened and how to avoid such tragedy again. Chair Thomas H. Kean, Republican and former governor of New Jersey, and Vice Chair Lee H. Hamilton, Democratic Congressman from Indiana, explained that the Commission had "reviewed more than 2.5 million pages of documents and interviewed more than 1,200 individuals in ten countries ... and nearly every senior official from the current and previous administrations ... and held nineteen days of hearings and took public testimony from 160 witnesses."

The Commission reported on its findings, without dissent, in 2004. It made a number of recommendations intended to strengthen our intelligence timeliness and quality. Some of them were that:

- the Director of Central Intelligence should be replaced by a National Intelligence Director to oversee national intelligence on specific subjects of interest across the government and manage the intelligence program and oversee the agencies that contribute to it;

- rebuild capabilities, better sharing of information between agencies;

- execution of paramilitary operations would be a DOD responsibility;

- total moneys spent for intelligence should no longer be kept secret: Congress should pass separate appropriations for intelligence;

- each house of Congress should have a single intelligence committee which combines authorizing and appropriating; and

- each house should have a single point of oversight and review for Homeland Security.

The Administration and Congress will grant the agencies more funds for more resources. All intelligence groups will reexamine how to better share what they know.

Yet we must be careful that information does not become too concentrated. A leader needs to read more than one newspaper, no matter how capable the editor. An American can read the *New York Times* and balance it with the *Wall Street Journal*. Each has worthy stories and views that are not in the other.

"Able Danger" was a code name for a terrorism research project set up in 1999 by US military intelligence of the Special Operations Command in Florida.

The group had been collecting information about Mohamed Atta, later identified as the 9/11 leader, who is believed to have been piloting the Boeing 767 which crashed into the North Tower. Months before the attack, the project group detected that he was in New York. They believed that the FBI should take him in. Other data revealed that Atta had a green card; as a legal visitor he was entitled to certain civil rights. No action was taken. Congressman Curt Weldon charged that Able Danger credibility was ignored and squelched.

A whistle-blower suit by a released FBI employee charged coverup. Attorney General John Ashcroft asserted "state secrets privilege" on the basis that litigation would risk disclosing sensitive national security information. The case was dismissed.

There could be records of some intelligence information which, if integrated with others, might have been significant. If Able Danger info had been followed up, would it have made a difference? Time will tell.

Critics allege government incompetence for failure to prevent the attacks. Ever since the attack on Pearl Harbor in 1941, politicians, scholars, conspiracy theorists, and skeptics still debate whose fault it was that the December 7th Sunday morning attack came as a surprise.

Now 9/11 conspiracy ideas abound: The government knew all about it before it happened. The Administration planned it. Ground-level explosives, not aircraft fuel fires, brought the buildings down. There are discussion groups, writers, and film makers who will pursue these ideas. Media coverage will give them credibility.

What should have been done prior to 9/11? Whose fault is it? What should be done about it? The debate is just beginning.

To facilitate sharing of information, Congress approved establishing the office of Director of National Intelligence directed by John Negraponte. He reports through the National Security Council to the President and monitors the budgets of virtually all US intelligence offices, including the CIA, headed by General Michael V. Hayden; the FBI, headed by Robert S. Mueller; the NSA, headed by General Keith B. Alexander; and the intelligence functions of the Army, Navy and Air Force.

The arrangement involves some dual reporting to assure cross-sharing of information. The dual reporting carries dual responsibility: a department leader risks assuming that "the other guy" has the problem resolved or "both guys" duplicate efforts. The office of Director of National Intelligence can be expected to regularly remind all intelligence organizations that they not waste energy on sibling rivalries, but instead focus on the common enemy.

Mindful of possible legal liability and/or desirous of preserving reputations, relevant leaders understandably are careful about what they say. Fault finding will continue. Attacks by fanatic terrorists will not stop.

CHAPTER THIRTEEN

Homicide

The Olson case had long been simmering below the attention of the national media radar. But the family was still seeking more truth about their father's death. There were two stories about how Dr. Olson went through the window and down to his death. In one, the companion said he had seen him run toward the window. In the other, his companion said he had been asleep and awakened by breaking glass. Both stories were ascribed to the same person, Lashbrook. Which was right?

With characteristic, extraordinary determination, the Olson brothers, Dr. Eric Olson, PhD, 50, and Dr. Nils Olson, DDS, 46, concluded that the only way to resolve the mystery was to disinter their father's body and have it examined by a team of independent forensic experts. After their mother died in 1993, they had the body exhumed.

Professor James E. Starrs, of the Institute of Forensic Science at George Washington University, led a team of fifteen forensic experts to examine the remains in 1994. They found no evidence of lacerations which might have been expected from breaking through a window. They did find evidence of a possible blow to the head, not likely to have been caused by the fall.

Members of Starrs' team—some, not all—concluded that the death of Frank Olson was not suicide, but homicide.

Some time after this forensic investigation, the Olsons discovered a CIA assassination manual which outlined how to assassinate someone and make it look like an accident. Suggestions included such methods as dropping a body 75 feet or more, having first gotten the victim intoxicated, drugged or stunned.

The brothers retained Attorney Harry Huge to persuade Manhattan, New York, District Attorney Morganthau to reopen the case. In early 1996, the DA assigned it to his new cold-case team. Obtaining clear answers would take some time.

The Olsons learned new insights from intelligence insiders.

Gordon Thomas, author of *Journey into Madness* and thirty-seven other books which sold 45 million copies, wrote an open memo in 1998 to Eric Olson about Frank Olson. Thomas's works drew upon his many years of probing the hidden world of secrets, intelligence, and disinformation. He wrote of the late Dr. William Sargant, a consultant psychiatrist of London, and Bill Buckley of the CIA, both of whom had known Dr. Olson. Thomas recalled that Sargant said he believed that Olson's soul-searching might make him a security risk, and Sargant passed this on to organization authorities. Thomas remembered that Sargant opined that "the staged death was almost classic." Buckley told Thomas that Richard Helms and Sydney Gottlieb are "experts in hiding and destroying evidence."

Though overshadowed by events of 9/11, the Olson case earned some attention in 2002. The Olsons were ready to be very explicit about the story of their father's death. They held a press conference on August 8 in Frederick, Maryland to proclaim that the death of their father "was a murder, not a suicide." They also said:

> *This is not an LSD drug-experiment story, as it was represented in 1975. This is a biological warfare story. Frank Olson did not die because he was an experimental guinea pig who experienced a 'bad trip.'*
>
> *He died because of concern that he would divulge information concerning a highly classified CIA interrogation program called 'ARTICHOKE' in the early 1950's, and concerning the use of biological weapons by the United States in the Korean War.*
>
> *The truth concerning the death of Frank Olson was concealed from the Olson family as well as from the public in 1953. In 1975 a cover story regarding Frank Olson's death was disseminated. At the same time a renewed coverup of the truth concerning this story was being carried out at the highest levels of government, including the White House. The new coverup involved the participation of persons serving in the current Administration.*

An untold number of articles have delved into the Olson case, and many will follow. There are several fine books. A compelling documentary movie premiered in Bremen, Germany, in August 2002. Egmont R. Koch and Michael Wech produced *Code Name: Artichoke, the CIA's Secret Experiments on Humans.* On camera are people who know what went on. It supports the Olson brothers' charges. Spokesmen for the US government apparently have made no comment about whether they have seen the movie or not.

The sons of Frank Olson, who were just nine and five years old when the government informed them that he had committed suicide, now, a half century later, are tired. They spent their youth emotionally drained by the official story. They have dedicated much of their adult years, their time and personal funds, to pursuing the truth and trying to force the government to admit its responsibility.

Who made the decision to dose Olson with LSD? Perhaps it was decided by a colleague—or was it planned by his supervisor? With or without advance approval by the unit?

After his condition became serious, who approved his separation and pension terms? What was the level of the person who authorized taking him to New York?

Why the quick trip south to Washington, DC, with his initial companion and then his almost immediate return back to New York with a substitute escort, Lashbrook? How high a level person in the CIA was tracking and/or deciding what to do?

In the 1950's, the government had considered sponsoring the assassination of a foreign leader who was perceived as a threat to the US security. Could the government have considered the assassination of a US citizen who was perceived as a threat to US security?

It is unlikely that any minutes of meetings, telephone conferences, or conference notes exist which could answer these questions. New York City authorities finally dropped the case. Insufficient evidence, it was said.

Those associated with the death of Frank Olson are deceased. Many of those who have stonewalled the revelation of the truth are still alive. And some of those are still in positions of significant power.

Now what? This case may never go away. Believers in justice will not forget Frank Olson. History will not forget Frank Olson.

Perhaps our national skepticism will change. America's mood and beliefs could shift. "The media" is a powerful force, which can make a difference. Credible, trustworthy leaders can make a difference as they wrestle with issues of secrets and disinformation.

CHAPTER FOURTEEN

Secrets

Researcher Robert Donaldson has continued a TWA 800 investigation started by his late brother, Retired Navy Commander William Donaldson, founder of the Association of Retired Aviation Professionals (ARAP). He believes that the official investigation produced an "environment of suspicion and distrust in the government's motives and conclusion.... Throughout all of this, they have ignored and tried to discredit more than 100 eyewitnesses who saw a streak, or fireworks rise from the surface and impact Flight 800."

How can more than 100 eyewitness accounts be ignored? What was that mystery boat? Why have these questions have been shunted aside? Why would our government want to keep the answers secret?

Our free society is nurtured by the right of free speech. Instead of holding our opinions quietly inside, Americans are free to sound off. We challenge the credibility of government statements. If we are concerned about the integrity of our leaders, we say so.

The powers that be can and occasionally do decide that it is important to keep the truth secret. What is hidden? Who decides? Why?

Our elected leaders swear to uphold our Constitution, ratified more than 200 years ago, which was ordained to "establish

Justice, insure domestic Tranquility, provide for the common defense, promote the general Welfare, and secure the Blessings of Liberty to ourselves and our Posterity...."

Over the years, our country has had many secrets, particularly during times of war. Germany was pursuing atomic energy as a weapon. We did not want Germany to know that we were determined and able to beat them to it. The Manhattan Project was cloaked in secrecy as we refined uranium and developed atomic weapons.

In the 1950's, the CIA sponsored development of the high-flying U-2 spy plane which would take photographs of activity in the USSR which the Russians did not want us to see. The project was hidden from prying eyes while designed and tested by Lockheed in Nevada. We did not want the Russians to know its altitude, speed, and range so that they would be incapable of shooting one down when it came over.

Use of chemical and biological weapons (CBW) had been virtually banned throughout the world. Yet Japan, Germany, the USSR, and the United States had active research projects in the 1940's and 50's. Besides learning how to create CBW, the research might also produce possible antidotes for anthrax, plague, and what the enemy might be doing.

In 2006, the US government announced that it would build an entirely new supersecret facility at Fort Detrick. It is believed that scientists inside will be researching ways to understand and defend against virulent and contagious agents which could affect large areas of our population. The new facility would have tight security to prevent the escape of dangerous substances and organisms. And we could expect very tight procedures to prevent the escape of secret information.

Much of the game is trying to stay ahead of the other side. Each wants an edge about which the others don't know. As Francis Bacon wrote, "Knowledge is Power." Special knowledge gives the holder special power.

John Le Carre, the ingenious spy novelist, has said, "History keeps her secrets longer than most of us. But she has one secret that I will reveal to you tonight in the greatest confidence. Sometimes there are no winners at all. And sometimes nobody needs to lose."

President Harry Truman, once warned, "Secrecy and a free, democratic government don't mix." But we know that he practiced an exception; he carefully guarded his knowledge of the Manhattan Project up to the time in 1945 when he authorized the bombing of Hiroshima. A secret is special knowledge which is closely guarded. It can precede a decision and action. Those in military and weapons research believe that what they are doing is consistent with the Constitutional objective of providing for the common defense. They feel especially qualified to be doing what they are doing. They believe information about what they are doing must not be available to an enemy.

We make great efforts to discover what our enemies are doing. Even a clue to a policy, a process, or a plan can be very important for us to know about them. So, too, they want to know about us. We try to protect our unique secret information. Anyone who jeopardizes our tight security lid degrades our nation's strength. The leaders of secret projects believe that their power must continue so that they can have the freedom of action and decision-making capability to further the project. Secret projects tend to perpetuate their secrecy. The importance of a secret can degrade over time, yet keepers of the secret can use complex controls and cause great expense to keep the lid on.

Sometimes secrets become part of a conspiracy. *Conspiracy* can be described as two or more people who are planning something which may be illegal. *The American Heritage Dictionary* definitions include: "An agreement between two or more persons to commit a crime or accomplish a legal purpose through illegal action." People who suspect possible coverups by the government are sometimes belittled as "conspiracy theorists."

A coverup requires disinformation—a misleading story, a credible story, intended to distract attention from the truth. The *Glomar Explorer* ship was publicly described as a research vessel which could extract resources from the bottom of the ocean. However, it is very doubtful that the Russians were fooled by this disinformation because they knew quite well that their submarine had sunk in the area where *Glomar* was probing the bottom of the ocean.

The official TWA 800 verdict appears to be intentional disinformation to conceal the real story which might have been an admission of US weakness or inability to protect airliners from surface-launched missiles. The dosing of Dr. Frank Olson with LSD made it appear that he was sufficiently deranged to commit suicide, but Dr. Olson's family believes that was only a cover story of how the government caused Dr. Olson's death so that he would not reveal the dark secret of American research and experimentation with chemical and biological weapons. Some people suspect that the conclusions of the Warren Commission about the killing of President Kennedy were primarily intended to calm down a clamor to attack Cuba, which might have led to war between the United States and the Soviet Union.

Ben Franklin said that three people can keep a secret if two are dead. If too many people know the truth, it is very difficult to keep the lid on, unless the full power and methods of government can be brought to bear. Favors and rewards can be promised for silence. Yet someone, somewhere, might leak the truth.

To cover up or not to cover up? That is the question.

We wonder where comes authorization or license to lie? Who will benefit from the decision? What will be hurt by the decision? Is the decision truly for the good of the country? Sophocles saw it as more than a black-and-white choice. He said, "Truly, to tell lies is not honorable; but when the truth entails tremendous ruin, to speak dishonorably is pardonable."

Little misdeeds at low levels of government are ignored or covered up if the consequences are minor. The biggest challenge to our society is when the coverup involves an incident of great significance and the decision to disinform involves persons at the highest levels and positions of power and authority.

The decision to classify something secret and to withhold the information can involve ambivalent and contradictory factors. There must be systems and procedures to prevent any person from making such a decision without checks and balances. Power, hunger for power, and pursuit of power cannot be allowed to run without restraints. George Washington warned, "The only maxim of a free government ought to be to trust no man living with power to endanger the public liberty."

In any organization, people of high-level authority and power tend to lose sight of their obligation to balance their personal benefits with the public benefits. It is a rare person in public office who does not enjoy the heady sense of power and control. Of course a certain amount of power is essential to accomplish good things. Some seek power because they want the respect and benefits that a position of authority provides. Power, rather than accomplishing something truly useful, is their goal.

Today insufficient attention is paid to the ethical issue of conflict of interest. A person elected to serve the public must, first and foremost, recognize and practice a fiduciary responsibility. As he acquires more power, his motivations can blur. Hiding behind the veil of secrecy is tempting and can lead to abuse of power.

Self-survival is a basic raw instinct. Civilization fosters ethical behavior. Power or pursuit of power can dilute ethical behavior. For many, a person's role is his identity. If he loses that role, he loses his sense of self-importance. If he perceives a threat to his role he will resort to defensive means of self-protection. Protecting his own position may transcend protecting the interests of those whom he serves. He may forget that the resources and powers that he controls belong to the people that he represents and are not his personally. It is unfortunately true that "Power corrupts, and absolute power corrupts absolutely" (with apologies to Lord Acton).

Some of those at high levels are tempted to hide some of their selfishness behind coverups. The techniques may involve misleading statements, bribing critics with reward or status, intimidating foes by arranging retribution, or obstructing justice by withholding information or not cooperating with those raising valid questions. Thomas Jefferson said, "When a man assumes public trust, he should consider himself public property."

The public needs to be on guard about abuses of power and conflicts of interest of its leaders, who may deem the security of their positions or party to be more important than their responsibility to the public.

Term limits could insure turnover in office and thereby prevent incumbents from building too much of a security wall around themselves. Turnover can also bring in new ideas. More than one voter casts his vote to oust the incumbent, to "throw the rascal out," and to give someone else a chance. Term limits would prevent an office holder from becoming too entrenched, too impressed with his own importance, and too focussed on his next election campaign.

Members of Congress, who are elected for two-year terms, are constantly campaigning for reelection. This causes them to stay close to their constituents, but it severely erodes the time they need to develop, analyze, deliberate and enact good legislation. US Senators have six-year terms, but are permitted to run for reelection. There are some who have been reelected into their dotage. A US President is barred from succeeding himself at the end of two four-year terms. He is in office long enough to learn how to do the job, but not so long that he gets out of touch with reality.

The State of Virginia allows a governor to serve four years after which he must step aside. Election to another four-year term must wait a minimum of four years. Virginia is traditionally one of the better managed states.

The challenge is to allow an office holder time enough to learn the job and develop enough relevant wisdom to run the government properly. Service too short leads to government by naive rookies. Service too long leads to complacency and sluggishness and arrogance. The topic of term limits deserves more consideration.

Our system grants significant authority to our elected officials, be they local, or county, or state, or federal government. These officials can require you to pay taxes. They can probe into your private life, your medical history. They can send a SWAT team into your house.

Who do you want to be your leaders? John Adams, who followed Washington as President said, "Liberty cannot be preserved without a general knowledge among the people ... who have a right, a divine right to that most dreaded and envied kind of knowledge ... of the characters and conduct of their rulers." For whom do you vote? What do you know about them? How do you know it?

Congress is a check on the Executive. The free press is a check on both.

CHAPTER FIFTEEN

Persuaders

In our democratic republic, the media exercises the right of free speech and orchestrates the national mind in ways unforeseen by the writers of our Constitution. The traditional media organizations grew, merged, and became concentrated and powerful. However, the Internet, with its disorganized worldwide instant accessibility, is a "new" media, sometimes competing with and critical of the "old."

It is no accident that as providers of entertainment and news, the media shape opinions and attitudes. The free press needs to be independent of government. It can spotlight malfeasance and abuse of official power. Government reveals only what it must and often spins what it can. Media probes for more. Proud of its watchdog status, it decides what it believes is "in the public interest." By omission, it decides what is *not* in the public interest. As in the childhood game of King of the Mountain, media is ready to bring down the high or mighty, and stands poised to attack on the smell of blood about issues and candidates.

Most news or analyses you see and hear have been selected from many sources and screened before it gets to you. Media digs up information, buys information, and receives tips or information fed to them. The process is like a funnel. Information is everywhere and overabundant. Reports can originate anywhere in the world—from regulars and free-lancers paid by publishing or news services—or from a flood of news releases pushed by government, businesses, or other organizations advocating a point of view—or anonymous tips—then through the editorial screens for veracity or relevance or interest. The editors set the filters. It is editors who can determine what you will see and hear. Finally it is sent to you, in print or broadcast over the air or the Internet.

News services like Reuters, Bloomberg, and Associated Press (AP) gather and supply stories and pictures from around the world. AP, the largest general news service, is a co-op owned by 1,500 newspapers. It has 3,700 employees at 240 bureaus throughout the world, who gather and supply news to 5,000 radio/TV outlets, 1,000 radio affiliates and 1,700 newspapers, 24 hours a day, seven days a week. The same story can appear on a network TV station in Wichita or on the pages of New York's *Newsday*, or be quoted on National Public Radio.

Tom Curley, president of AP, said, "The most important thing from our standpoint is to connect what we do to the public interest, and to line up with the people and remind them how important it is that they get access to what their elected representatives are doing."

By the end of the twentieth century, most of what the public read and heard came from the traditional mainstream media (MSM), composed of ten large organizations led by executives who ultimately decide what would go to the public.

The ABC network has claimed that more Americans get their news from ABC than any other source. The MSM includes the eight most influential newspapers (*USA Today, Wall Street Journal, New York Times, Boston Globe, Los Angeles Times, Newsday, Chicago Tribune,* and *Washington Post*) owned by five companies; seven most-watched TV networks (ABC, CBS, NBC, Fox, CNN, TNT, ESPN) owned by another four companies; and two most widely read magazines (*Time* and *Newsweek*) owned by two of the same companies. These ten MSM firms include Disney and Time Warner who also create and promote movies for TV and theaters. These firms own 110 TV stations. These MSM organizations are big businesses, and like other big industries, such as oil or autos, they are led by executives not chosen by public vote.

The broadcast media gets income by selling air time (higher price for prime time) and print media get income from selling space (higher price for the best spaces). Broadcasters tend to allocate more time to what is exciting or entertaining than what is important information. Entertainment programs win over news. Reporters and advertisers are star-struck by celebrities, be they entertainers, athletes, or villains. Each week we are told which movie outsold which other movie.

There is media self-promotion and absorption. Gossip and job changes become the news: there was widespread coverage of the question—would Katie Couric go to CBS or not? CBS spent weeks promoting her first newscast. The hype seemed to imply a coronation, almost befitting the inauguration of an elected leader. There are stories of how the TV crew managed to get a picture at an event. On radio newscasts, the announcer frequently says his own name more than he says the name of the subject of the story, justifying the criticism that newscasters are entirely too self-important.

Too infrequently the reporter digs into historical background to help the public better understand issues. Too little time is available. Cable channels' instant reactions to breaking events can misreport facts because of insufficient research and confirmation. Rare is the commercial broadcaster who permits a Mike Wallace to peel off the veneer of a news release. It seems that most of what the public gets are trivia or brief burps of information.

News stories are often constructed from quotes of people who witnessed an event or made things happen or from interesting citizens or cognizant officials. This method risks that a witness may have the facts wrong. The official or organizational spokesperson may omit or twist the facts to convey what his superior wants the public to know. Experienced reporters have learned to be skeptical of public statements.

Journalists and investigators would be well advised to develop more skill in analyzing finance and accounting. Congressman Otis Pike, when probing the CIA in 1975, concentrated on the Agency budget and how tax money was used. The CIA resisted, knowing that beneath each number was something to be explained. Historians Will and Ariel Durant said "men who can manage money manage all." The money trail is key to understanding much of what happens in the world. Where did it come from? Who received it? Has the flow changed? Who has the official power to regulate it? Following the money trail within a solid knowledge of history enables a journalist to describe an event in perspective and help the public understand the issues.

When reporting malfeasance, the media need consider the observations of Patrick Buchanan, who was communications director for the Reagan Administration during the Iran-Contra affair and saw how zealous were the attacks on Ronald Reagan and, later, when he himself was a candidate for the presidency. He cautions:

> *The media does not just expose wrongdoing, they revel in it, rejoice in it, profit from it—as it enables them to preen as morally superior to those hapless souls whose sins and scandals they have uncovered.*

President Teddy Roosevelt said it another way: "Men with muckrake are often indispensable to the well being of society, but only if they know when to stop raking the muck." Too much attacking of our leaders undermines the public respect for duly elected authority. It also breeds reportorial arrogance and deters good people from serving in public office.

The media's influence on issues is profound. It is not surprising that the results of survey polls of public opinion match what the media has been proclaiming prior to the survey. If more coverage of positive aspects of the US life were reported, the polls of public satisfaction would be more positive.

America On Line (AOL), with almost 20 million Internet users, is part of the giant Time Warner corporation whose annual $45 billion business includes publications, broadcasting, music, and movies. Such breadth of scope enables one part of the company to help promote another part. An AOL news page may include a picture of an actress appearing in a Warner-produced film. Synergy has cost benefits, but it inhibits open availability of objective information. "Sixty Minutes," a CBS TV news program, granted interview time for the author of a book which was published by a sister company. There is no measure of how much these cross-support activities leave fewer resources for competitors or for objective news.

As we all know, political contests can be close games. Here is where publishers and broadcasters can make or break a political figure as they decide which newsmaker gets the most print space or air time and which picture is selected—the grimace, the silly expression, the exuberant scream, or the confident, likable face. Each candidate hungers for a newspaper's formal endorsement.

An elected official can schedule a press conference, but there is no assurance that a reporter or a news camera crew will be assigned to be there or that the story will actually air.

The media gets the last word—unless a candidate pays for it with a lot of money for display ads, direct mail, or TV spots. The media wins either way. They editorialize or "endorse" and/or they collect advertising dollars.

Top media executives are well paid and enjoy social parity and rapport with political leaders or play golf with corporate moguls. They tend to be gentle when criticizing companies which provide needed advertising dollars. They relish gibing "big business," but they rarely criticize their own businesses. They believe that their own values are good, right, and noble. Mindful of the power they exercise in shaping US and world opinion, the top managers of these organizations consciously try to be objective and fair in their coverage of events and issues. Nevertheless, they are human, with foibles, and their bias subtly affects how they choose who to entrust with managing daily affairs of their company and with deciding the choice of stories (who decides whose face will be *Time*'s cover this week?). Not so subtle is the tilt of their editorials.

In spite of their power over the public mind, the media moguls are not scrutinized the way government leaders are. They do not hold press conferences and allow penetrating questions. They are not available for comments any hour of the day wherever they are. They are not hounded by reporters and photographers. Unlike elected officials, they can enjoy very private lives.

They have risen to the top of their profession through coincidence, skill, talent, hard work, and by building favorable relationships. They, like politicians, exercise power and enjoy the benefits of access to power. These people shape the mind of America, but voters did not "elect" them in the usual way.

The "votes" that put them in place and keep them there are readers, viewers, listeners and dollars—from advertisers and subscribers. Consumer boycotts are negative votes which can reduce that income.

Because the media determines much of what we know about issues and events, the large media organizations must be on guard that they do not abuse the power that they enjoy. The boards of media giants need to be cognizant of their responsibility to the nation's well-being and be on guard against conflicts of interest. It would be a brave media executive who would analyze, critique or report on the unchecked concentration of power in his industry or corporation.

Influential people of power and accomplishment are invited to share their wisdom and serve on elite boards as trustees or directors. Vacancies are chosen by the management and the existing board. This precludes dramatic changes of policy. They like the fees for attending meetings, and they enjoy learning from the other influential people who serve with them. Each trustee, director, or executive has a fiduciary responsibility to protect the interest of the share owners of the organization he serves. He needs to avoid what William F. Pounds, dean emeritus of the MIT Sloan School of Business, cites as "individual self-interest, to the detriment of what others might think of as the general good."

CHAPTER SIXTEEN

Mind Teams

As we move into the twenty-first century, the clout and influence of the MSM is declining. Newspaper readership is shrinking as internet usage is growing. The "new" or "alternative" Internet media grows with hundreds of thousands of independent reporters, picture-senders, thinkers and advocates, uninhibitedly exchanging ideas on the Internet. It is a disorganized giant library with no walls, an information center, growing daily. The Internet provides news and info any time of day.

Veteran anchor Jim Lehrer has said that everyone should get their news however they want to and in whatever form they want.

The avenues of Google, AOL, Yahoo, and hangouts like MySpace are drawing viewers, especially younger people, away from television. Interaction and instant reporting provide spontaneity unmatched by staid, formal media organizations. As a result, the traditional MSM companies are testing ways to participate in and benefit from the internet global phenomena.

Media leaders gathered in 2006 at a Sun Valley, Idaho, retreat to learn from each other and perhaps form new alliances. The invitees included key executives of providers such as News Corp, Time Warner, Yahoo, Viacom and Google; and advertisers such as Nike and Coca Cola. They watch each other and hope to participate in the fast-changing new technology mediums of iPods and wireless phone/computers.

The "new media" is a disorganized anarchy of unregulated ideas and information which is changing what we can know. Thousands, or maybe millions, of volunteer participants supply the Internet's vast information cafeteria of everything from jewels of fact, to important ideas, varied opinions, and misinformation junk food.

With his computer, a user can build his own "newspaper" from sources he likes. He can read it, listen to it, add to it, print it out.

The very speed of the Internet is its peril: unlike printed media, which is usually checked and rechecked, much internet information has not been subjected to serious scrutiny before it is posted for millions to see. Ronald Reagan would remind web users that trust is fine, but also verify.

Search engines access millions of web sites, blogs, journals, archives, and hourly news reports. Wireless phones and e-mail offer the opportunity to connect with people of common interests or concerns. A group becomes like a super brain. People from anywhere in the world combine their experience, their unique knowledge, and their analytic skill into a giant brain, with strength greater than its separate parts. They may never meet face to face, but they collaborate to pool their wisdom, hoping to help truth emerge.

Two common-interest groups exemplify what the free Internet mind building makes possible: The Association of Retired Aviation Professionals (ARAP) and Flight 800 Independent

Researchers Organization (FIRO) have each researched and analyzed the tragedy of the destruction of TWA 800 for almost a decade. Both have concentrated on building the case that a missile did it. They have not been focussing on whose missile(s) did it. FIRO members include an electronic engineer in Massachusetts, a veteran 747 captain in California and a lightning expert in the South. The results of group efforts and mutual support confront the barriers of the government.

An individual can probe the bureaucratic haze to search for the truth without the help of the media. President L. B. Johnson, on Independence Day 1966, signed into law the Freedom of Information Act (FOIA). The Department of Justice advises that under the FOIA "all federal agencies" are generally required "to disclose records requested in writing by any person. However, agencies may withhold information pursuant to nine exemptions and three exclusions contained in the statue. The FOIA applies only to federal agencies and does not create a right of access to records held by Congress, the courts, or by state or local government agencies. Each state has its own public access laws...." FOIA helps open the door to government information, but just a crack.

TWA 800 researchers have invoked FOIA procedures. Hundreds of objects or fragments were removed from TWA 800 victims for forensic analysis which might reveal the presence of warhead explosive or rocket chemical elements or rule them out. Results were not made public. Graeme Sephton, an electronic engineer and FIRO volunteer, exercised FOIA channels to get the FBI to release the results. He filed a FOIA request to the FBI for information about the analysis. When information was not forthcoming, he brought suit against the FBI. In court, the FBI did not claim an exemption, but indicated they could not find what he wanted. The first court hearing agreed with the government. He appealed. The next higher court again agreed and accepted the FBI position that it had a made a good-faith effort and was unable to comply with the FOIA request. There is no ready answer to explain if the results were lost, misfiled, or if the evidence itself was lost.

If there was no evidence of explosive chemicals or rocket propellants, it would strengthen the NTSB verdict of a spark being the cause of the TWA 800 explosion. Failure to reveal the results of forensic analysis leaves the impression that the government either didn't care to find out or it did find out and it does not want us to know what they found. Suspicion remains.

FIRO persists in pursuit of information about a key piece of evidence which could show that TWA 800 had been hit by a missile. In July 2006, FIRO filed a lawsuit n US District Court in Boston to force the NTSB to respond to its FOIA requests since 2004. Scientist Dr. Tom Stalcup, head of FIRO, charges that the government is concealing and denying the existence of a key piece of evidence which had exited the airframe at apparent supersonic speed and had been recovered, but has since been unaccounted for. As of this writing, the court decision is pending.

The CIA asserted that what many witnesses thought were missile streaks were instead burning fuel trailing behind the broken plane as it climbed after the initial explosion. The CIA prepared an animation which showed the plane's nose being blown off and then the plane climbing upward 3,000 feet, trailing burning fuel. Capt. Ray Lahr concluded that laws of physics and aerodynamics would prevent such a climb. Using

FOIA, he requested that the CIA show how they calculated such a climb. They refused to comply. He took them to court. As of this writing, the case has not been resolved. FIRO members believe that the streaks that had been seen were tracks of a missile or missiles and not a rising trail of burning jet fuel. Failure to reveal the method of calculations as the basis for the climb leaves suspicion that it cannot be substantiated.

Although there are FOIA exclusions and exemptions, a citizen can inquire and get a response. In some cases, the government response is that it can neither confirm nor deny that it has relevant information. FOIA does not assure that the government will reveal what it does not want to reveal.

Unless the decision violates our inalienable principles of personal and private rights, government can make some things secret. To defend against enemies, the US needs to guard information which could strengthen the enemy's ability to hurt the US. To maintain domestic tranquility, the US needs to sedate the availability of some information which might trigger catastrophic rioting or panic behavior.

The ARAP and FIRO web sites have had more than a million visitors and have incorporated more and more details which help establish what really happened to flight 800. The power of the evidence and the power of the analyses may yet persuade a whistle blower to speak out. Richard Nixon once erected an information stone wall, expecting that in time probers would give up and go away. Truth did come out. There is no known FOIA success so far of uncovering a "smoking gun" of culpability or illegal act in the TWA 800 case. Yet.

Events of 9/11 will be intensely scrutinized in the years ahead. Opponents of the Administration will find evidence of procedural or personal inadequacies. Conspiracy theories will flourish. And while voices in our free society joust with each other, real enemies will be scheming new attacks on America.

CHAPTER SEVENTEEN

You Choose

The Whistle Blower Protection Act of 1989 seemed to offer hope as a way to expose improper or illegal acts. But in 1997 Bill Clinton showed that a President could void its protections by issuing an Executive order. Then in 2006, the Supreme Court added a clarification which may further deter some potential whistle blowers. The Court ruled that the "blowing" cannot be part of an official communication. Justice Anthony Kennedy, for the majority, wrote that "Official communications have official consequences.... [An employee's official communication] ...needs to be accurate, demonstrate sound judgment, and promote the employer's mission."

If a blower were to step out of his role as an employee and speak as a private citizen, it might be impossible for him to be perceived as free of his official aura. He will be very vulnerable.

Whistle Blower laws and FOIA are only two roads to revelation. A private citizen, or a group of citizens, can use the internet as an information highway. The most potent force for transparency is media.

The new media can go forth to sample life that goes on outside of courthouses and government buildings, to talk to people when they are not playing a role, to talk with them when they are being themselves.

But the MSM is particularly well postured to do what the new media cannot: initiate inside stories about more people and more places of power. Government and large organizations manage their reputations with professional public information officers, carefully written new releases, and staged public relations events, while reminding their employees not to bite the hand that feeds them. The public is well served when big MSM counterbalances big P.R.

A media executive could use his power and high level relationships to dig behind the veneer of prepared news releases and press conferences. He could—but he might not do so if it would tarnish the image of people he personally supports.

It is media that chooses what news to offer to you in your paper, on your radio and on your TV. If you rely on the same newspaper every day, the same magazine, or the same radio, TV. or news web site, you are vulnerable to subtle bias. You have been keeping the media "in office" by reading, watching and buying what their sponsors offer. To protect your mind, you too should choose where and how you get your news. You can vary your news diet.

There are alternatives available. Search for a well-rounded, balanced news diet. Put your time and your money on services or sources that are right for you. Choose carefully where you get your information. Explore unfamiliar sources to strengthen your mind and your understanding.

Your vote at the polls is vitally important to our country and our way of life. Choose carefully who you vote for.

We are not a pure democracy where we vote on every issue. An often forgotten fact is that the United States is a republic. In a republic, the voters elect people to represent them, and they make decisions affecting the voters. It would be impractical to hold a public referendum to decide every significant issue. Your government representatives and the people they appoint decide the issues and the rules of our society. Important issues are being decided every day in Congress, in the White House, in the courts, and in administrative and regulatory offices.

It is tempting to complain about "those politicians in Washington" or "those in the State capital." They are there because they were elected or because someone who was elected put them here. Thomas P. "Tip" O'Neill, Jr., Massachusetts Congressman, served ten years as Speaker of the House. He saw many issues come and go, many officials rise through the system. He famously observed that "all politics is local." Virtually all top level leaders start out at a low level and then rise from there. Otis Pike served on the Riverhead, New York, Town Council and as a local Justice of the Peace before being elected to Congress. After being reelected six times, he rose to chair the important House Select Intelligence Committee. George Allen started as a state delegate. Then he became a state senator. Then a governor of a state. Then a US Senator. He may even try a run to be President. The people in your locality may someday hold high office.

The most profound decisions are made at the highest level by many who began their political careers at the local level in a community or neighborhood like yours.

Major decisions are shaped by the character and the values of the people making those decisions. Can your representative resist the temptations that power attracts? Will your representative put the country's good above his own interest?

And finally every voter need ask himself this: "Am I careful about who I vote for?" Learn all you can about the candidates, what they really believe, what they really stand for, who they really are. Good government starts with you in your local voting booth.

There will always be secrets. There will always be coverups. There will be leaders who are wise and leaders who are not.

This little book has been a history, a selection of certain perplexing, mysterious events of the recent half century that are of importance to us all.

A history combines pieces of information, but it is a jigsaw picture with some pieces peculiar and some pieces missing. What the picture shows depends upon the historian. Broadcaster Red Barber recalled overhearing a great baseball umpire say, "It's not a ball and it's not a strike: it's nothing until I call it." History itself is an umpire too. When all has been said and written, and enough time has passed, History will decide what was so.

Until then, the search for the truth will continue.

Acknowledgments

This book is based upon public information, concepts, ideas and facts learned while living. I salute the courage and dedication of all those who push for truth.

Kind and competent people who shared their ideas, experiences and insights include Mike Bouvier, John F. Carr, Boyd Claytor, Anne Cline, Bob and CDR. Bill Donaldson, Cong. Virgil Goode, Michael Hull, Jack Jennings, Dr. Tom Jennings, Capt. Ray Lahr, Andy Larson, Corky Meyer, Capt. Al Mundo, Mike Nichols, David Neal, Dr. Eric Olson, Capt. Carl Overstreet, Lacey Putney, Mike Rivero, Ernie Ryan, Graeme Sephton, Tom Shoemaker, Dr. Tom Stalcup, and George Stewart. Thanks also to former boss Jack Bierwirth who sent me hither and yon to broaden my understanding of finance and the world and to colleague Weyman "Sandy" Jones who advised how to work with the media.

I thank my special mentors: Dick Hutton ("write as though you had to pay for each word"), Clint Towl ("never make a threat unless you are ready to go through with it"), Lew Evans ("adults are only older children") and ("people act on the way things seem, not as they are"), and Bill Pounds ("leaders act a role"). My wife, Cyndi, helped hone my thinking and kept me going.

I am especially grateful to Judge William M. Sweeney and lexicographer Anne Soukhanov for reviewing the draft and offering constructive suggestions.

And thanks to Amy G. Moore for formatting the text and for designing the cover.

Authors I have read and the people with whom I have spoken are not responsible for my interpretations, opinions, errors and conclusions. Mistakes are mine alone.

                                              Peter Viemeister
                                              Bedford, Virginia, 2006

More Information

PRINT

Aircraft Accident Report: In-flight Breakup Over the Atlantic Ocean — Trans World Airlines Flight 800 — Boeing 747-131, N93119 — Near East Moriches, New York — July 17, 1996, National Transportation Safety Board, 2000.

Altered Evidence: Flight 800: How and Why the Justice Department Framed a Journalist and His Wife, James D. Sanders, 1999.

Crossfire — The Plot That Killed Kennedy, Jim Marrs, Carroll and Graf Publishers, 1990.

The Death of a President, William Manchester, Harper and Row, 1967.

"Detective Said Scientist Had 'Severe Psychosis'," Joseph B. Treaster, *New York Times*, July 11, 1975.

Disinformation — 22 Media Myths That Undermine the War on Terror, Richard Miniter, Regnery Publishing, Inc., 2005.

The Downing of TWA Flight 800, James Sanders, Kensington Publishing Corp., 1997.

"A Father Lost: Son Probes Strange Death of WMD Worker," Scott Shane, *Baltimore Sun*, September 12, 2004.

First Strike — TWA 800 and the Attack on America, Jack Cashill and James Sanders, WND Books, 2003.

In the Blink of an Eye — The Investigation of TWA Flight 800, Pat Milton, Random House, 1999.

JFK and Sam — The Connection Between the Giancana and Kennedy Assassinations, Antoinette Giancana, John R. Hughes, and Thomas H. Jobe, Cumberland House, 2005.

Killing Hope — US Military and CIA Interventions Since World War 2, William Blum, Common Courage Press, 2005 edition.

Into the Buzzsaw: Leading Journalists Expose the Myth of a Free Press, ed. Kristina Borjesson, Prometheus Books, 2002.

The Lessons of History, Will and Ariel Durant, Simon and Schuster, 1968.

The Lightning Book, Peter E. Viemeister, MIT Press, 1972.

The 9/11 Commission Report, National Commission on Terrorist Attacks Upon the United States, W.W. Norton & Co., 2004.

Red Star Rogue — The Untold Story of a Nuclear Submarine's Strike Attempt on the U.S., Kenneth Sewell with Clint Richmond, Simon & Schuster, 2005.

Report of the Warren Commission on the Assassination of President Kennedy, Warren Commission, McGraw-Hill Book Company, 1964.

Robert Kennedy and His Times, Arthur M. Schlesinger, Jr., Houghton Mifflin Company, 1978.

Rogue State: A Guide to the World's Only Superpower, William Blum, Common Courage Press, 2005 edition.

Rush to Judgment: A Critique of the Warren Commission's Inquiry into the Murders of President John F. Kennedy, Officer J.D. Tippit and Lee Harvey Oswald, Mark Lane, Holt Rinehart & Winston, 1966.

The Secret Team: The CIA and Its Allies in Control of the United States and the World, L. Fletcher Prouty, Bandit Productions, 1997.

"Suicide Revealed," Thomas O'Toole, *Washington Post*, June 11, 1975.

A Terrible Mistake — The Murder of Frank Olson and the CIA's Secret Cold War Experiments, H.P. Albarelli, Jr. and John Kelly, to be published in 2006.

Thirteen Days, Robert F. Kennedy, W.W. Norton & Co., 1969.

TWA 800: Accident or Incident, Kevin E. Ready and Cap Parlier, Saint Gaudens Press, 1998.

Years of Lyndon Johnson, Vol. 2, Means Of Ascent, Robert A. Caro, Alfred A. Knopf, 1990.

INTERNET — www.

JFK-Info.com

archives.gov/research/jfk/search.html

twa800.com   (Associated Retired Aviation Professionals)

flight800.org   (Flight 800 Independent Researchers Organization — FIRO)

ntsb.gov/events/twa800   (National Transportation Safety Board)

9/11commission.gov

frankolsonproject.org

transparencyinternational.org

wikipedia.com

MOVIES and TELEVISION

JFK, Directed by Oliver Stone, Based on works of Jim Marrs and Jim Garrison, 1991.

Code Name Artichoke: The CIA's Secret Experiment on Humans, Egmont R. Koch and Michael Wech, Egmont R. Koch Filmproduktion, C. Bertelssman Verlag, 2002.

Unsolved History: JFK Conspiracy, Discovery Channel, 2003.

Index

ABC, American Broadcasting Corporation 126
AOL, America On Line 129
ARAP, Assoc.of Retired Aviation Professionals 117, 134
ATF, Alcohol, Tobacco and Firearms 89
Able Danger 108
Abramson, Harold 8, 22-25, 29, 66
Abu Nidal 77
abuse of power 122
Achille Lauro 79
Accuracy in Media 90
Acton, Lord 123
Adams, John 124
Aegis System 80
Afghanistan 72, 78-80
Agnew, Spiro 55
Alexander, Keith B. 110
Al Qaeda 77, 106
Allen, George 141
American Heritage Dictionary 120
Angelides, Paul 86

anthrax 118
Apollo Program 42
Arab-Israeli War 54
Area 51 (Nevada) 32
Armstrong, Neil 11
Artichoke, Code Name 113
Ashcroft, John 109
assassination 31, 41, 48, 66, 112
Associated Press 126
Atta, Mohammed 108
Australia 79
Ayatollah Khomeini 72

Bacon, Francis 37, 119
Back to the Future 11
Baghdad 82
Bantam Books 45
Barber, "Red" 142
Batista 30
Bay of Pigs 39
Beatles 49
Beck, Dave 28
Begin, Menachen 72
Beirut 73
Bin Laden, Usama 77

149

biological weapons 19
blogs 134
Bloomberg 126
Blum, William 65
Boeing 85, 92
Boggs, Hale 44
Boland Amendment 74
bomb threats 53
Boston Globe 126
Bouvier, Mike 36
Breshnev, Leonid 55
Britain 21, 79
Brumley, Dwight 86
Brown vs *Board of Education* 27
Buchanan, Patrick 128
Buckley, Bill 112
Bush, George H. W. 68, 74
Bush, George W. 105

CBS, Columbia Broadcasting System 126
CBW, Chemical Biological Warfare/Weapons 19, 60
CIA, Central Intelligence Agency 17, 37, 55, 65, 106, 128, 136
CNN, Cable News Network 85
Calverton, NY 87

Carter, Jimmy 66
Casey, William 74
Castro, Fidel 30, 41, 47, 66
Chamberlain, Neville 98
Chamorro, Violet 76
Cheney, Richard 55, 62, 68
Chestnut Lodge 41
Chicago Tribune 126
Church, Frank 56, 64
Clarke, Richard 88
Clinton, William J. 83, 100, 139
Coca Cola 133
"Code Name Artichoke" 113
Colby, William 62, 68
Cold Spring Harbor Laboratory 23
communism 27
conflict of interest 131, 122, 132,
Conally, John 45
conspiracy 64, 120, 138
Constitution, US 31, 73, 117
contempt citation 63
Contras 74
Cooper, John Sherman 44
Couric, Katie 127
Cronkite, Walter 11
Cruise Missiles 82
CSI 13
Cuba 27, 121

150

Cuban Missile Crisis 40, 97
Curley, Tom 126
Cyclone Class Ships 97

DCI, Director of Central Intelligence 107, 110
DIA, Defense Intelligence Agency 106
DOD, Department of Defense 108
Dallas 43
DaVinci Code 11
Democratic Convention 52, 83
Desert Storm 82
Detrick, Fort/Camp 17, 62, 118
Dillon, Douglas 56
disinformation 68, 120
Disney 127
Donaldson, Robert 117
Donaldson, William 101
Drone 95
Dubs, Adolph 72
Dugway Proving Grounds 60
Dulles, Allen 21, 44
Dulles, John Foster 21
Durant, Will and Ariel 128

ESPN 126
Edgewood Arsenal 23
Egypt 79
Eisenhower, Dwight David 20, 36
Ellsburg, Daniel 54
Embassy, US-Iran 72
Embassy, US-Libya 72
executive orders 44, 66, 100
Export-Import Bank 92

FAA, Federal Aviation Agency 93, 98
FBI, Federal Bureau of Investigation 37, 86, 106, 110, 135
FIRO, Flight 800 Independent Researchers Organization 99, 134
FOIA, Freedom of Information Act 68, 135
Feminine Mystique 49
fiduciary 122, 133
Ford, Gerald 44, 55, 62
FISA, Foreign Intelligence and Surveillance Act of 1978 65
Franklin, Benjamin 121
Friedan, Betty 49

Germany 18
Giancana, Antoinette 64
Giancana, Sam 13, 31, 64
Glomar Explorer 67, 120
Goode, Virgil 102
Google 133
Gorbachev 80
Gottlieb, Sidney 20, 22, 112
Graham, Katherine Meyer 41
Graham, Philip 41
grassy knoll 48, 59
Great Society 50
Grumman Corporation 7, 53, 87, 92
Gulf of Tonkin Resolution 50
Gulf War 87

Hall, James 31
Haines, Gerald K. 63
Hamas 77
Hamilton, Lee H. 107
Havana 29
Hayden, Michael V. 110
Helms, Richard 112
Hersh, Seymour 55
Hezbollah 73
Hills, Rodney 61
Hiroshima 119
Hitler, Adolph 31
Hoch, Paul 29

Hoffa, Jimmy 28
Hoover, J. Edgar 37
Hormuz, Strait of 85
hostages 72
House Select Intelligence Committee 63
Huge, Harry 112
Hughes, Howard R. 67
Humphrey, Hubert 52
Hunt, E. Howard 59
Hussein, Saddam 81

Illinois election 35
International Military Tribunal 19
Internet 14, 134
Iran 21, 99
Iran Air 80
Iran-Contra 73, 128
Iraq 80, 81
Iraq-Iran War 80
Iron Curtain 32
Irvine, Reed 90, 101
iPod 134
Islam 78, 79
Israel 51, 71, 93

Japan 18
Jennifer Project 67
Jefferson, Thomas 123

Johnson, Lyndon Baines 27, 44
Jordan 79

Kallstrom, James 86, 92
Katzenbach, Nicholas 50
Kean, Thomas H. 107
Kennedy, Anthony, Supreme Court Justice 139
Kennedy, Jacqueline Bouvier 35
Kennedy, John Fitzgerald "JFK" 13, 35
Kennedy, Joseph Patrick 27
Kennedy, Robert F. 28, 50, 71
Kennedy, Ted 28
Khalid Sheik Mohammed 83
Khobar Towers 84
Khruschev, Nikita 33, 55
King Kong 11
King, Martin Luther Jr. 49
Kirkland, Lane 56
Kissinger, Henry 59, 63
Koch, Egmont P. 113
Koran 79
Korean Conflict 20 62, 113
Kuwait 79, 81

Lake, Anthony 85
LSD, Lysergic acid diethylamide 20, 22, 49, 113
Lahr, Ray 91, 136
Lansky, Meyer 30
Lashbrook, Robert V. 24, 61, 114
Leary, Timothy 49
Lebanon 74
Le Carre, John 119
Lehrer, Jim 133
Lemnitzer, Lyman 56
Libya 72, 79, 81
lightning 91
Lockerbie 81
Lockheed 32, 118
Los Angeles Times 67, 126
Lyons, Robert 40

MSM, Main Stream Media 126, 133, 140
Macy, Josiah Jr. Foundation 29
Maddox, USN 50
Mafia 43
Manhattan Project 118
Manila Plot 83
Marcy Park 14
Matthews, H.L. 30
MBNA Bank 93
McClelland Committee 28

153

McCone, John A. 37
McCoy, John S. 44
McDougal, Jim and Susan 83
McNamara, Robert S. 36, 40
media, new 125, 134
media, old 125
Meyer, Katherine (Graham) 41
Meyer, Corwin "Corky" 92
Meyer, Eugene 41
Meyer, Frederick 86
mind warfare 21
MIT Sloan School of Management 7, 132
MKULTRA 21
mob 28, 41
Monroe, Marilyn 14
Moon Program 39, 42
Moorer, Thomas Admiral 101
Morganthau, Robert 112
Morse, Wayne 50
Mossadegh, Mohammed 21
Mueller, Robert S. 110
Mujahideen 81
Mundo, Albert 91
Munich Olympics 93
Muslims 72
MySpace 133
mystery boat 93, 117

NTSB, National Transportation Safety Board 86, 90
NSA, National Security Agency 106
NSC, National Security Council 74
National Public Radio 126
National Security Act 37, 100
Naval Special Warfare Development Group 100
NCIS 13
Nedzi, Lucien 56
Negraponte, John 110
Newsday 126
Newsweek 127
New Yorker 88
New York Times 7, 15, 45, 53, 55, 84, 106
Nicaragua 74
Nike 133
Nine/Eleven (9/11/2001) 38, 103, 138
Nixon, Richard M. 20, 30, 46, 69
North, Oliver 74
North Korea 20
Nurenberg 19

OPEC, Organization of Petroleum Exporting Countries 54
oil 78
Olson, Frank, Alice, Eric, Lisa, Nils 14, 17, 61, 111
Olympics 72, 83, 93
O'Neill, John 88, 103
O'Neill, Thomas P. Jr., "Tip" 141
Oswald, Lee Harvey 13, 42, 46
Oswald, Marina 42
Overstreet, Carl 12, 32

P-3, Lockheed patrol airplane 95
Pakistan 79
Palestine 71
PanAm 81, 103
Parlier, Cap 99
Pataki, George 93
Pavlavi, Shah 21, 72
Pearl Harbor 103, 109
Pennsylvania Hotel 24
Pentagon Papers 54
Pike, Otis 56, 76, 128, 141
PLO 77
plausible deniability 75
Poindexter, John 75
Pounds, William F. 132

power, pursuit of 121
Powers, Gary 33
Prouty, L. Fletcher 37

Ramzi Ahmed Yousef 83, 84
Rankin, J. Lee 44
Ray, James Earl 51
Ready, Kevin E. 99
Reagan, Ronald 56, 66, 72, 128
Rensselaer 7
Reuters News Service 126
Richmond, Clint 68
Rivero, Michael 97
Rockefeller, Nelson 55, 56, 59
Rome 91
Roosevelt, Franklin D. 28
Roosevelt, Theodore 129
Roselli, Johnny 64
Rosenthal, A. M. 54
Ruby, Jack 42, 46
Rumsfeld, Donald 55, 62, 68
Rusk, Dean 37, 40
Russell, Bertrand 46
Russell, Senator Richard 18, 44
Russell, Richard (pilot) 90
Russia 32, 39, 80, 118
Ruwet, Vincent L. 23

SEC, Securities & Exchange Commission 28
Sadat, Anwar 72
Salinger, Pierre 88, 101
Sandanistas 73
Sanders, James and Elizabeth 89
Sargant, William 22, 112
Saudi Arabia 78
Schultz, George 74
secrecy 38, 62, 64, 117
separation of powers 63, 73, 76
Sephton, Graeme 135
Sewell, Kenneth 68
Shah (see Pavlavi, Shah) 21, 72
Shakespeare, William 12
Shi'a Sect of Islam 73
sheep 60
Sirhan, Sirhan 51, 71
Sixty Minutes 129
Skunk Works 32
Smith, Bedell 21
Sommer, Mike 90
Sophocles 121
South Korea 20, 80
South Vietnam 27, 79
Stalcup, Tom 99, 136
Stark, U.S.S. 80
Starrs, James E. 111
Stennis, John 65
Stevenson, Adlai 21

Stinger missile 81, 84, 86
Stone, Oliver 13
Sturgis, Frank 59
submarine 67
Sulzberger, Arthur Ochs "Punch" 53
Summa Corporation 120
Sunni Sect of Islam 78
Supreme Court of US 54, 139
Sureté 86
SWAT team 124
Syria 72, 79

TWA 800 7, 84, 96, 130, 135
TWA 847 80
Taliban 81
Tehran 72
term limits 123
terrorists 77
Texas School Book Depository 42
Thomas, Gordon 112
Time Warner Corp. 127, 129
Time Magazine 52, 127, 130
Tomahawk missile 82
Tonkin, Gulf of 50
Tower, John 75
Towl, E. Clinton 53

Trafficante, Santo Jr. 30
Treaster, Joseph B. (*NY Times*) 61
Truman, Harry S. 19, 119
Tucker, Jimmy Guy 83

U-2 planes 12, 32, 33, 118
UAE, United Arab Emirates 79
UN, United Nations 20, 71
USA Today 126
Usama bin Laden 77

Viacom 133
Viet Cong 51
Vietnam 27, 54
Vincennes, USS 80, 85
Virginia 134
Vito, Carmine 33
Vosper Thorneycroft 97

WBPA, Whistle Blower Protection Act 100, 139
Wallace, Mike 128
Wall Street Journal 106
Walker, Edwin A. 42
Walsh, Lawrence 73
Ward, James W. 61
Warren Commission 13, 44, 121
Warren, Earl 44

Washington, George 122
Washington Post 41, 60, 126
Watergate 54, 59, 69
Watson, James D. 23
Wech, Michael 113
Weinberger, Caspar 75
Weldon, Kurt 109
White House 88, 104, 113
Wicker, Tom 43
Woodstock 52
World Bank 41
World Trade Center 15, 83, 103
Wright, Lawrence 88

Yahoo 133
Yousef Ramzi Ahmed 83

Zawahiri, Ayman al 77

157